Siân Nolan

Siân's
Beaded Nee ses

Claudia Schumann
50126 Bergheim, Germany
http://www.Creanon.de
Info@Creanon.de

Concept and Jewelry: Siân Nolan
Text: Siân Nolan and Claudia Schumann
Photography: Claudia Schumann
Portrait on page 6: Jessica Macey
Layout: Claudia Schumann
Technical illustrations: Claudia Schumann
Editor for the English edition: Nathalie Mornu
Illustrations: © macrovector - Fotolia.com

Printed in Germany

ISBN: 978-3-940577-31-3

Table of Contents

Welcome

Fifteen or so years ago, my Mum bought me a beading kit for Christmas. It was a peyote-stitched needle case and was my first exploration into beads. So it seems almost perfect, and yet unbelievable, that I now find myself writing this book full of my very own needle case designs.

I love the whimsical and the unusual, so inside these pages you will find a fun collection of quirky, fun and contemporary cases perfect for holding your beading needles.

Some are more suited to decorating your desk, such as the Perfume Bottle, Darcey or Belle of the Ball, while others, like Hula Hoop and Skelly, with their fun movable parts, you won't want to put down! For more practical - yet still wonderful - designs, colorful cases such as Zigzag, Turkish Delights and Talini are perfect for keeping in your beading tool kit.

In closing, I just want to say a big "thank you" to my friends and family for giving me lots of encouragement and support throughout all my beady adventures.

Siân Nolan

Basics

Delica

All Delica (cylinder beads) are from *Miyuki* in Japan. They are very uniform in size and this ensures your beadwork will fit the needle cases.

Seed beads

All seed beads used are also from *Miyuki* in Japan.

Crystals

When it comes to radiance, Swarovski® is the premium brand. These crystals are the best quality and have the brightest sparkle.

Needle cases

All needle cases are made of wood with a diameter of 13 mm and a height of 6 or 9 cm. I recommend painting the needle cases in a matching acrylic paint before beading, and allowing them to dry before beading them.

Needles and Thread

I like to bead with needles from *Tulip* and I normally use size 10.
My favorite thread is K.O. in a matching color. This is a synthetic thread which is prewaxed and ready for use.

Transparent nylon thread

For some projects you will work with transparent nylon thread and a size 10 needle. To help thread your needle, flatten the end of the transparent nylon thread with a pair of pliers and position your needle only a few centimeters from the end of it.

Tools

At most, you need scissors to cut the thread.
For some designs, you'll need to poke a hole in the lid of the needle case. For this I use an awl from *Tulip*, but you can make the holes with a little hand drill.
For bending loops, you will need a pair of round-nose pliers. And for opening and closing jump rings, have on hand two flat-nose pliers.

Miscellaneous

I recommend a transparent glue.
Sometimes a piece of a double-sided tape is helpful; you can find it in a craft store.

The Base

If nothing else is mentioned, the base is worked in circular peyote. After every round you have to step up (stitch through the first added bead of the round).

Round 1 (6x yellow beads):
Pick up 6x Delica and close to make a circle.

Round 2 (6x green beads):
Add 1x Delica between each Delica.

Round 3 (12x dark blue beads):
Add 2x Delica between each Delica.

Round 4 (12x light blue beads):
Add 1x Delica between each Delica.

Round 5 (12x orange beads):
Add 1x Delica between each Delica.

Round 6 (18x pink beads):
At the corners (above the increase of round 3), add 2x Delica. For the sides, add 1x Delica between each Delica.

Round 7 (18x turquoise beads):
Add 1x Delica between each Delica.

The Body

Round 1 + 2

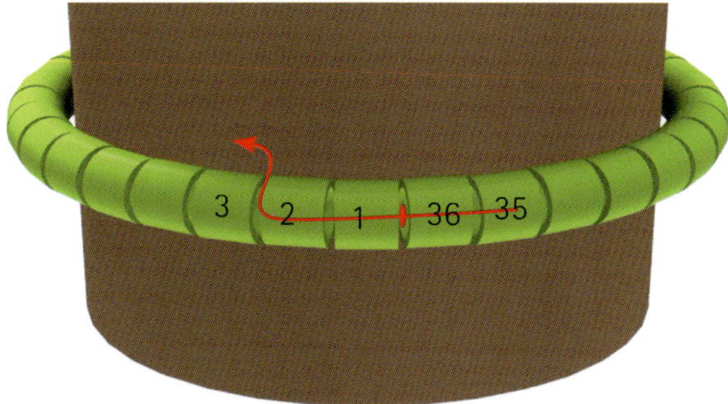

Round 3

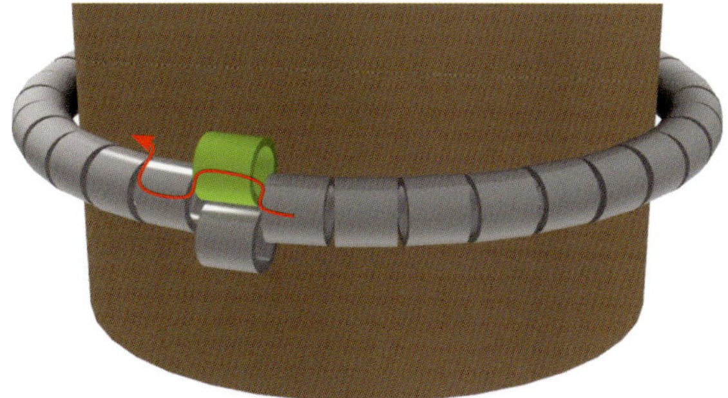

Round 4

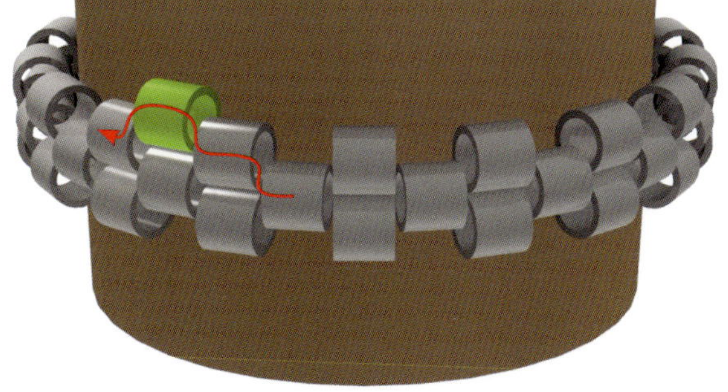

If nothing else is mentioned, the body is worked right to left, from the bottom to the top, in peyote stitch, following this pattern.

Round 1 and 2

The 36 beads of round 1 and 2 are picked up together. Secure the thread with a double knot and stitch forward, so your needle is coming out of the second bead added. (Also see page 11.)

Round 3

* Pick up 1x Delica, skip one Delica and stitch through the next Delica. Repeat from * all the way around.
To start the next round you have to do the step-up. To do so, stitch through the first bead added in this round (see next figure).

Round 4

Now you can see where the next bead has to be added - remember to do the step-up after every round.

Tip

If your beadwork is a little loose around the wooden case, you can wrap the case with some tape. I use surgical microporous tape.

The Join

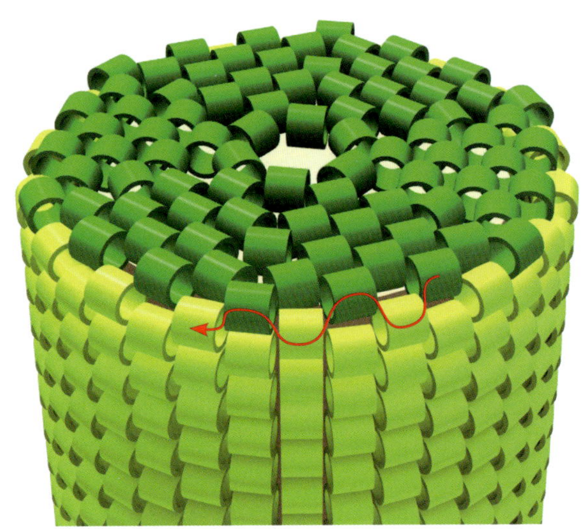

The beads of the base will align with the beads of the body, enabling you to just zip them together.

The Patterns

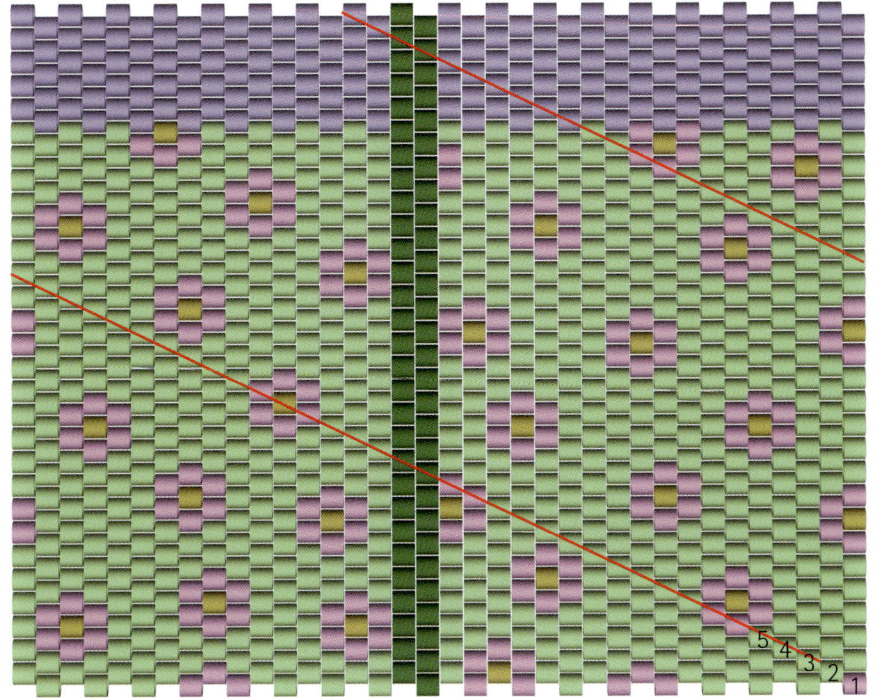

The red diagonal line marks the first bead of each round; this is also the bead through which you do the step-up. Because of the step-up, the starting bead advances one bead to the left each row.

Because we all work with a different tension and occasionally there can be slight differences in the size of the wooden cases, it maybe necessary to adjust the length of your work for a perfect fit. If the design allows, it is usually possible to add or subtract a row at either end of the pattern.

Patterns

Darcey, p. 58

Hula Hoop, p. 70

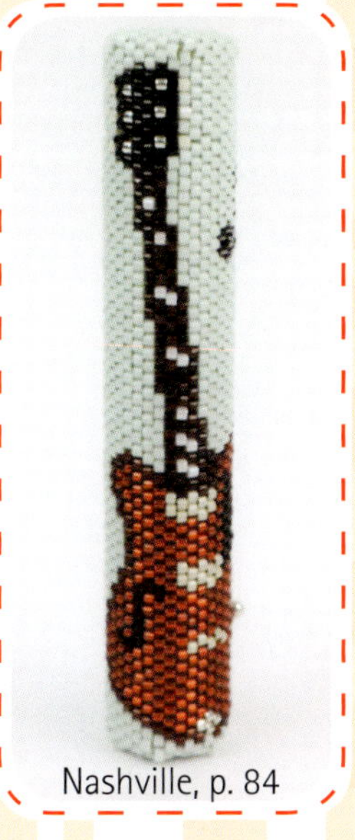

Nashville, p. 84

Zigzag, p. 52

Perfume Bottle, p. 62

Skelly, p. 79

Belle of the Ball, p. 88

Talini

MATERIALS FOR TALINI

CRYSTALS FROM SWAROVSKI

1	Rose Cut (2072), 12 mm, Crystal

BEADS

4 g	11/0 Delica, #0078 Pale Aqua
3 g	11/0 Delica, #0202 White
3 g	11/0 Delica, #1184 Magenta
2 g	11/0 Delica, #0463 Dark Fuchsia
1 g	11/0 Delica, #0607 Bright Teal
1 g	11/0 Delica, #0612 Smoked Topaz
1 g	11/0 Delica, #0205 Dark Flesh
8	11/0 Delica, #0070 Rose Pink
6	11/0 Delica, #0010 Black
3	11/0 Delica, #0362 Red
10 g	15/0 seed beads, #0420 White
37	Drops, 2.8 mm, #0420 White

OTHER

5	Crystaletts, 3 mm, silver setting, Crystal AB

Needle case, 9 cm
White acrylic paint
Glue
Double-sided tape

MATERIALS FOR THE CHARM

BEADS

1 g	11/0 Delica, #0202 White
1 g	15/0 seed beads, #0420 White (A)
1 g	15/0 seed beads, #4201 Silver (B)
31	Drops, 3.4 mm, #0420 White
62	Drops, 2.8 mm, #0420 White

OTHER

1	Wooden disc, 25 mm
1	Jump ring, 8 mm, silver
1	Mobile phone strap, Light Blue

Acrylic paint for skin, hair, eyes and cheeks
Thin red marker for the mouth
Matte acrylic varnish
Brush
Double-sided tape

Base

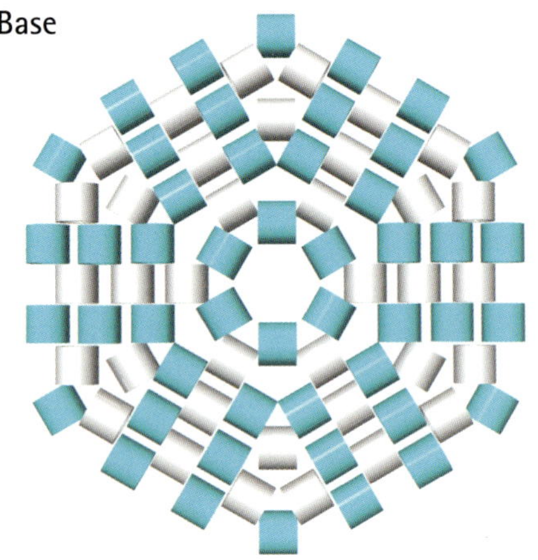

Lid

Base

Work the bottom following the diagram using Delica #0202 and #0078.

Body

Work the body starting at the bottom. The dark blue beads on the chart mark the places where you stitch in the drop beads for snow. The 10 red beads mark the positions where you add the Crystaletts. One Crystalett is worked in over two rounds; on the second round, don't add any new beads, just stitch through the existing Crystalett. The fur effect is added to the white Delica beads around the face, sleeves and coat. There is no "exact" way to do this. Work in a circular stitch by coming out of a Delica, picking up 2x or 3x 15/0 seed beads and then stitching back into the Delica, but from the other side. The beads creating the fur will give a 3D-effect and overlap each other.

Lid

Attach the crystal to the top of the lid either with double-sided tape or glue.
Work 12 rounds of the pattern and attach them with a little piece of double-sided tape to the wooden lid. Stitch three rounds of 15/0 seed beads in peyote. Work one more round, but this time add a bead in every other gap. Stitch through the beads of the previous round in between each new bead.

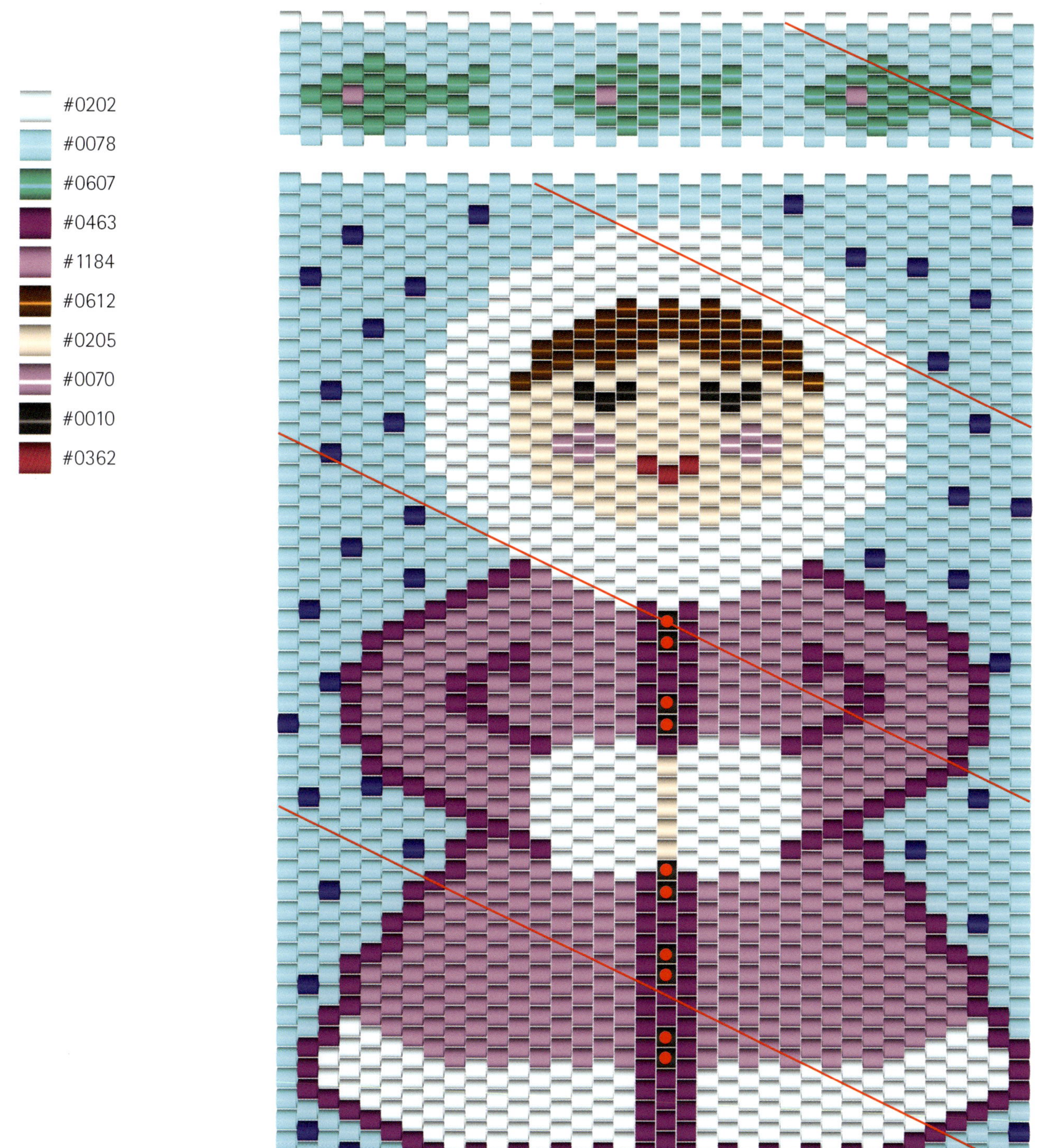

#0202
#0078
#0607
#0463
#1184
#0612
#0205
#0070
#0010
#0362

The scissor charm, preparing the face

At left, you see the face actual size. Use it as a guide to paint the wooden disc on both sides, then apply varnish. Let it dry.

General hints for the bezel

The bezel around the face is worked in peyote stitch using the two-needle start. This method is particularly useful when you are unsure how many beads you need for your bezel. It is easy to adjust the size to fit your disc exactly.
The figures show the bezel flat, without the wooden disc.

Figure 1

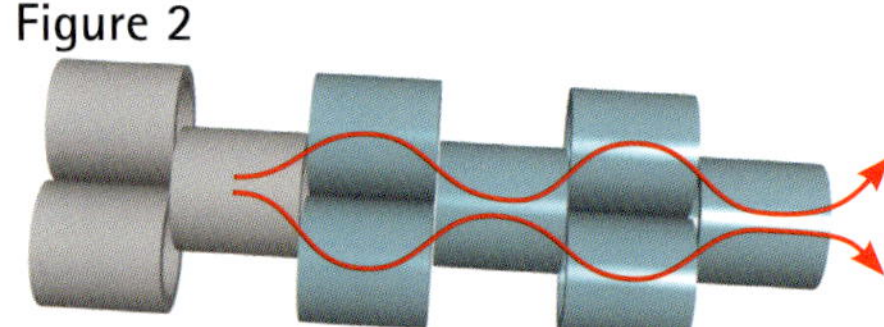

Figure 1

Pick up 1x 11/0 Delica on each needle and stitch through 1x 11/0 Delica with both needles. Slide this set of beads to the center of your thread so your working threads are the same length. This is the first unit.

Figure 2

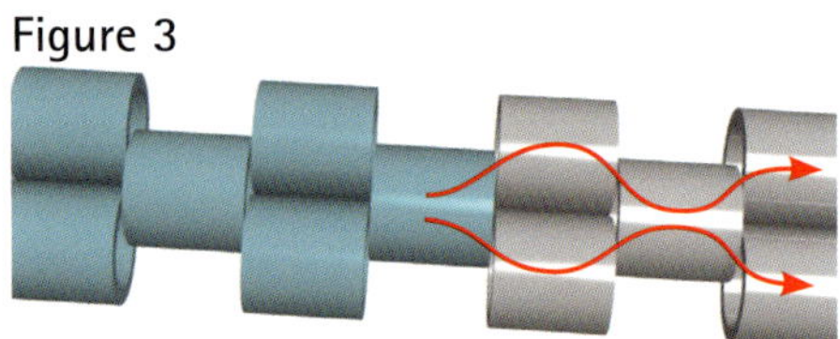

Figure 2

* Pick up 1x 11/0 Delica on each needle and stitch through 1x 11/0 Delica with both needles. Repeat from * until you have 31 units.
If your beaded band fits around the wooden disc you can go to figure 3. If your band is too long or too short, add or remove some units.
Note: A piece of double-sided tape at the edge of the wooden disc is helpful for keeping your work in place.

Figure 3

Figure 3

To join the beads into a circle, just stitch through the first beads as shown.
Now continue with one needle for each side.

Figure 4

Figure 4

With your first needle, work one round in peyote; don't forget the step-up.
With your second needle on the other side of your bezel, work one round in peyote, stepping up at the end of the row.

Figure 5

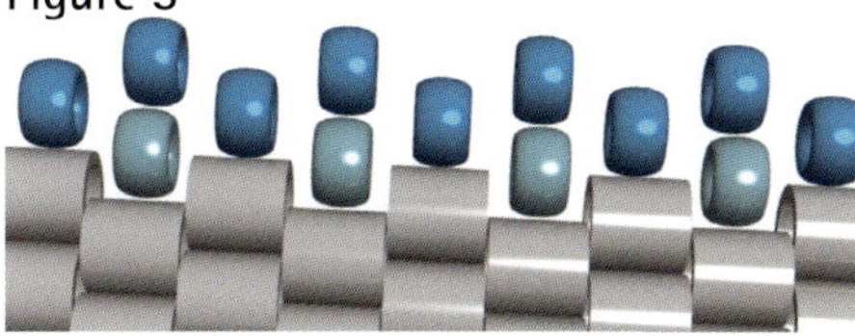

Figure 6

Figure 7

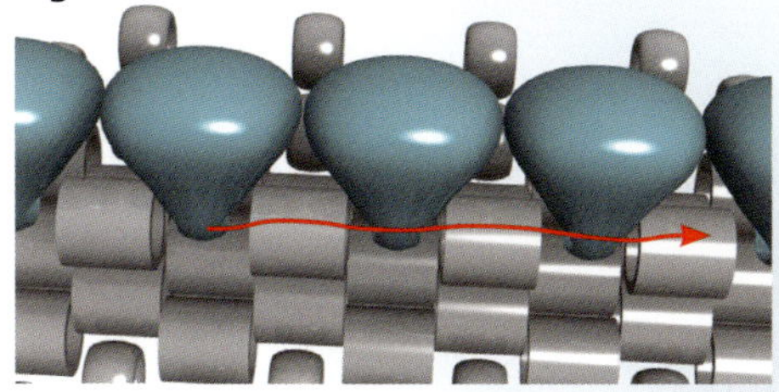

Figure 7a

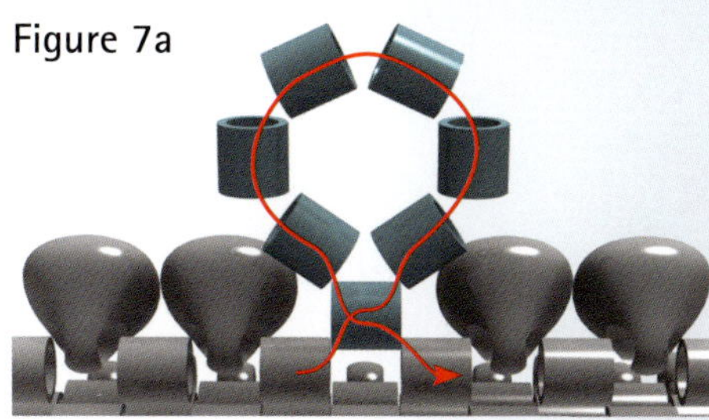

Figure 8

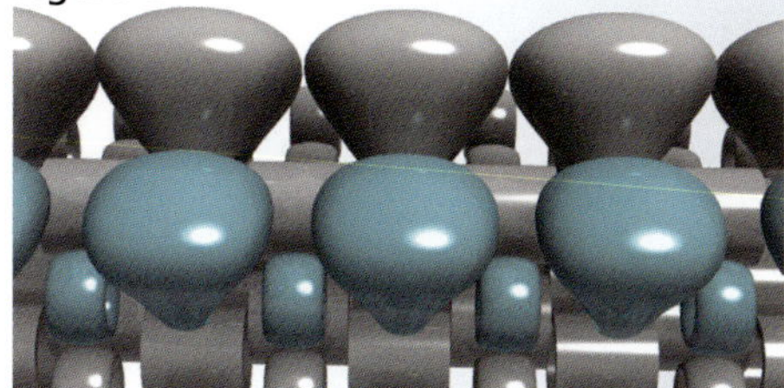

Figure 5

With each needle, work one round of 15/0 A and two rounds of 15/0 B seed beads (don't forget the step-up!). Pull your thread, so the face is bezelled.

Figure 6

Weave through the beads to exit the middle row of Delica beads. Pick up 1x 11/0 Delica and stitch through the next Delica ("stitch in the ditch"). Repeat this all around the wooden disc.

Figure 7

With your needle coming out of one of the Delica beads added in figure 6, pick up 1x 3.4-mm drop and stitch through the next Delica. Repeat this all the way around the wooden disc. When you get to the top of the face add a loop of 7x 11/0 Delica instead (see figure 7a). Reinforce the loop by going through all the beads again, then weave through so your needle is coming out of a Delica added in figure 4.

Figure 8

Add 1x 15/0 A seed bead between each Delica by stitching in the ditch as in figure 6. After this round, add 1x 2.8-mm drop between the 15/0 seed beads. Repeat this on the other side.

Finishing

Attach the jump ring of the mobile phone strap to the beaded loop.

Needle Ninja

Materials

CRYSTALS FROM SWAROVSKI

about 138 Flat Back (2058), SS10, Jet

BEADS

5 g	11/0 Delica, #0310 Black
1 g	11/0 Delica, #0774 Red
26	11/0 Delica, #0200 White
2	11/0 Delica, #0216 Cobalt Blue
18	15/0 seed beads, #0401F Black

OTHER

Needle case with cone, 6 cm
Black acrylic paint
Glue
Toothpick or cocktail stick

MATERIALS FOR THE CHARM

BEADS

1 g	11/0 Delica, #0310 Black
18	11/0 Delica, #0230 Gold
1 g	11/0 Delica, #0035 Silver

OTHER

2 cm	Chain (3 mm), silver
2	Toothpicks or cocktail sticks
2	Jump rings, 5 mm, silver
2	Lobster claws, 10 mm, silver
14 cm	Ball chain (2 mm), silver

Nylon thread, 0.25 mm, transparent
Sandpaper or nail file
Acrylic paint in black and silver

Body/Head

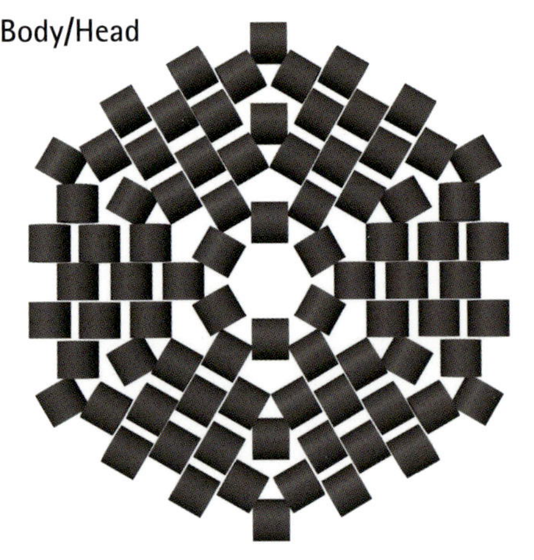

Base

Paint the cone black and let it dry. Glue on the flatbacks; to do this pick up a very small amount of glue with a toothpick and dab it on the black cone. Press the flatback in position very carefully.
Hint: You will probably have a tendency to use too much glue. It would be a good idea to test doing it on a piece of paper a few times.

Body/Head

Referring to the chart at right, work the body starting from the bottom. Once you have finished the peyote part made with Delica, add one round using 15/0 seed beads (these beads are colored gray in the chart at right).

Bandana (bow for the eyemask)

You will work the bandana separately (in brick stitch) and sew it to the head.

Figure 1:	First connect four beads with ladder stitch using Delica beads #0774.
Figure 2:	With your needle coming out of the outermost bead, pick up 2x 11/0 Delica and stitch under the thread lying between the two middle Delica. Stitch back through the last Delica added. The existing thread in figure 1 is colored green and the new one is colored blue.
Figure 3:	Pick up 1x 11/0 Delica and stitch under the old thread and back through the new Delica just added.
Figure 4:	Add two more beads to the left side then follow figure 4 to complete the bandana.
No diagram:	Work a second bandana and stitch the pieces together using a circle stitch through the edge beads. Then stitch to the top of the body/head.

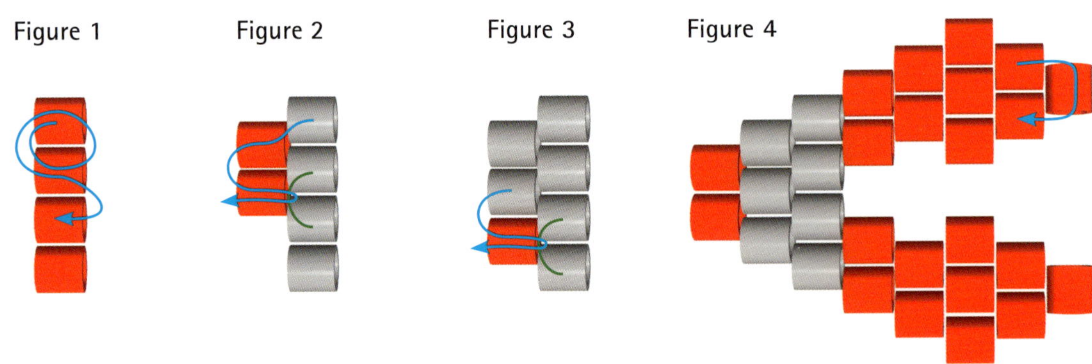

#0774
#0310
#0200
#0216

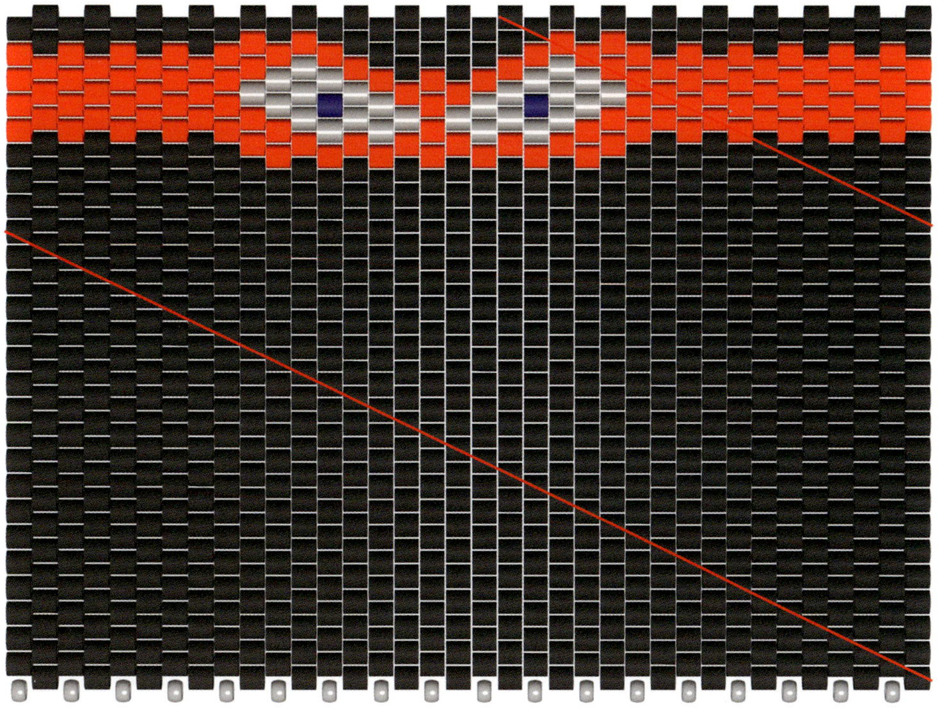

Figure 1

Katana (sword), figure 1

The body of the sword is worked in CRAW (see page 96). Don't stitch through the top four beads of every unit in this case; this will allow you to put in the toothpick later.

Note: The handle has gold Delica on only two sides!

Cut the toothpick so it is a bit shorter than the sword and slip it into the sword. If it doesn't fit, carefully rub with sandpaper. Pull it out, paint it with the silver and black acrylic paint, let it dry and put it back into the sword. Stitch several times through the four black Delica at the end and add 1x 11/0 Delica to the tip of the sword (see next figure).

Figure 2

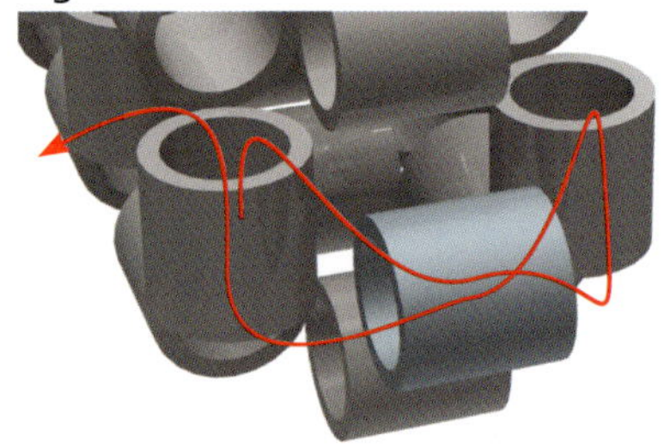

Figure 2

With your needle coming out of a Delica at the tip of the sword, pick up 1x silver 11/0 Delica and stitch through the opposite Delica. Stitch back through the Delica just added and the Delica your needle is coming out of. Sew in the threads and cut them off.

Tsuba (hand guard of the sword), figures 3 to 6

Starting from the last round of black Delica (marked with red dots in figure 1, and colored pink in figures 3 to 6), work the tsuba with nylon thread and two needles. When you have added all beads, stitch through the outer circle of Delica several times. Sew in the threads and cut them off.

Figure 3 Figure 4

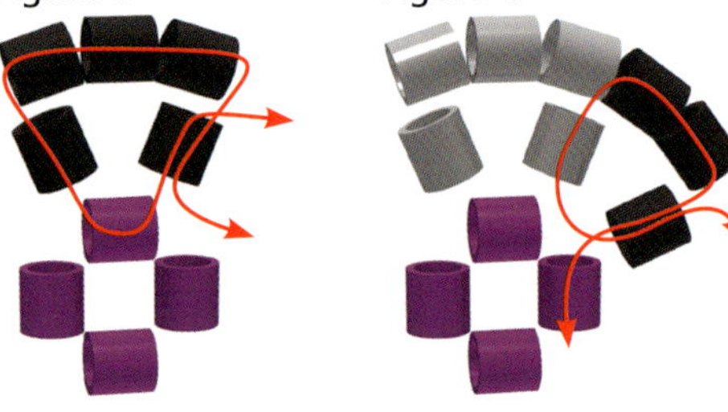

Figure 5

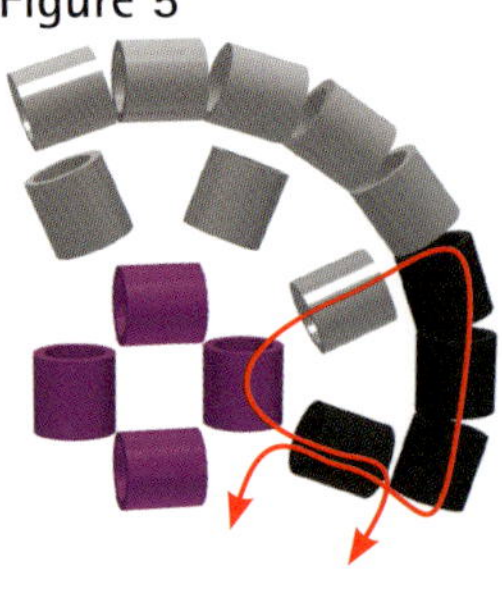

Figure 6

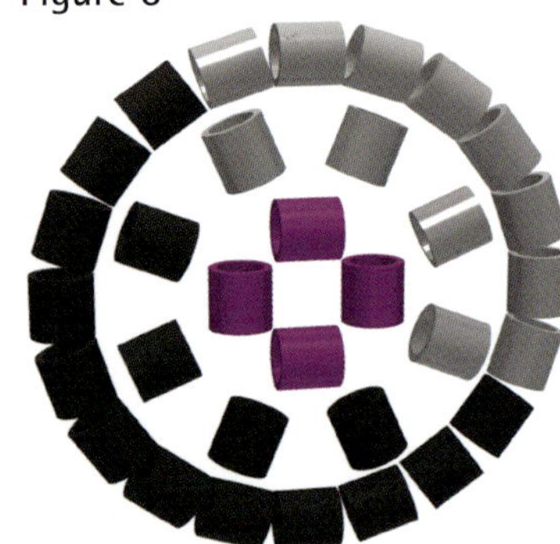

Figure 7

Nunchaku (nunchucks), figure 7

The nunchucks are worked in the same way as the sword. First make the body in CRAW (without closing the units on the top), then add a toothpick as you did for the sword. Stitch through the black Delica beads at the end several times.

Stitch through to the other end and sew on the first link of the 2-cm chain instead of a Delica as shown in figure 2.

Work a second nunchuck in the same way and sew it on to the other end of the chain.

Open the jump ring and insert into a link of the chain about half-way along and add the clasp.

Monika's Sheep

BEADS

7 g	11/0 Delica, #0169 Chartreuse
2 g	11/0 Delica, #0351 White
2 g	11/0 Delica, #0883 Cream
1 g	11/0 Delica, #0310 Black
30	11/0 Delica, #0202 White
10	11/0 Delica, #0200 White
11	11/0 Delica, #0160 Yellow
5	Drops, 2.8 mm, #0401 Black

OTHER

Needle case, 9 cm
Light green acrylic paint

OPTIONAL

1	Sheep bead made of glass
12 cm	Jewelry wire the same color as the sheep
1	Metal bead, about 3 mm
1	Crimp bead
1	11/0 seed bead the same color as the sheep

Flat-nose pliers
Awl

Base

Base

Work the base following the figure.

Body

Referring to the chart at right, work the body starting from the bottom. The beads marked with a red dot are the noses of the sheep; work them with the drops.

Lid

Work the lid using Delica #0169 and following the chart.

The optional sheep

If you are lucky enough to have a matching lampwork sheep bead, you can add it to the top of the lid.

To do this, make a hole with your awl in the middle of the wooden lid. Pick up a seed bead on the jewelry wire, then take both ends of the wire through the sheep (from back to belly) and through the lid. Pick up one or two metal beads; these act as spacer beads to allow room to maneuver the pliers. Pass both ends of the wire through a crimp bead; while pulling tight on the wire, flatten the crimp and cut off the excess wire.

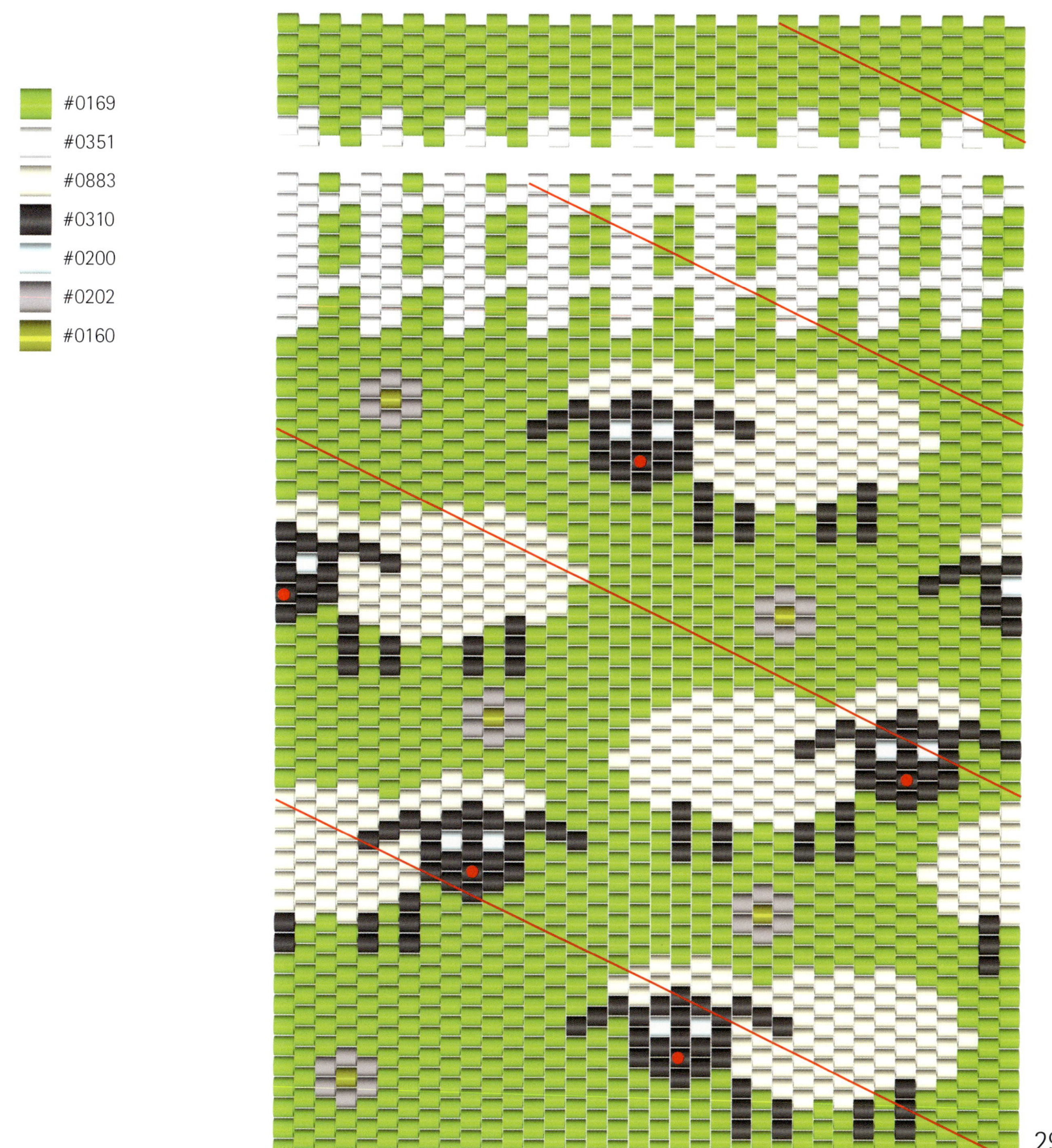
#0169
#0351
#0883
#0310
#0200
#0202
#0160

Emiko

CRYSTALS FROM SWAROVSKI

117	Bicones (5328), 2.5 mm, Tanzanite
30	Bicones (5328), 2.5 mm, Emerald
about 5	Bicones (5328), 2.5 mm matching the chignon

BEADS

5 g	11/0 Delica, #1182 Dark Mint
2 g	11/0 Delica, #0027 Green Teal
2 g	11/0 Delica, #0629 Lavender
1 g	11/0 Delica, #0624 Pastel Pink
1 g	11/0 Delica, #0331 Gold
9	11/0 Delica, #0732 Rich Cream

OTHER

1	Polymer head bead "Emiko," 15 mm
1	Needle case, 6 cm
4	Head pins
1	Metal bead, about 3 mm

Green acrylic paint
Flat-nose pliers
Round-nose pliers
Wire cutter
Awl

Base
Work the base with Delica #1182.

Body
Work the body from the bottom to the top following the chart.

Lid
Work the lid as shown in the figure below and in the chart.

Attaching the head to the lid
Poke a hole in the wooden lid with your awl. Using a head pin, pick up a metal spacer bead, and thread the head pin up through the lid from the inside. Add your Emiko head, then make a wire loop as close to the bead as possible (see page 97). To make the kanzashi (hair decorations), use two head pins; pick up 3x bicones on one, and 2x bicones on the other. Use round-nose pliers to make loops, then hang them from the eye of the first loop.
If your head spins too much, you can fix it in place with a little bit of glue on the inside of the lid - but if you do, make sure Emiko is looking in the right direction!

Obi
The explanation for the obi is on page 34.

Lid

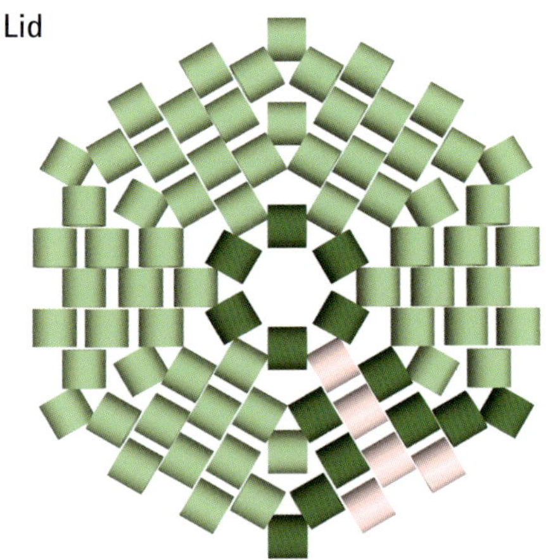

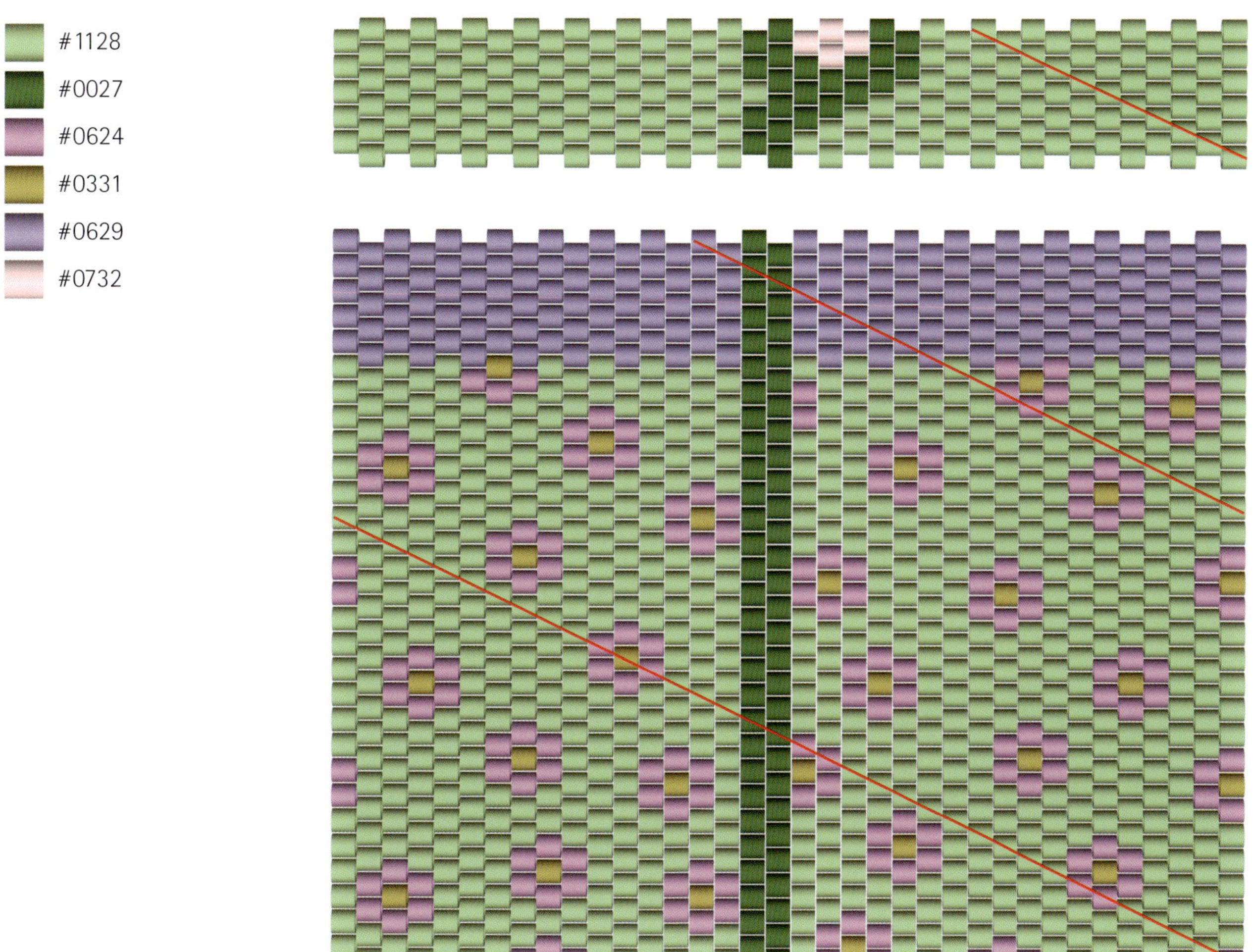
#1128
#0027
#0624
#0331
#0629
#0732

Figure 1

Figure 2

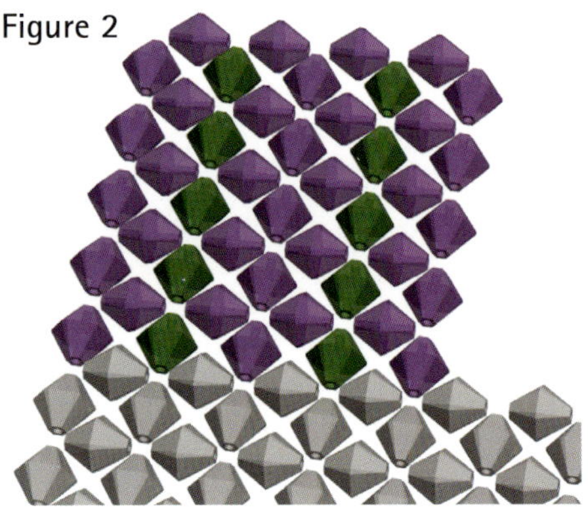

Figure 3

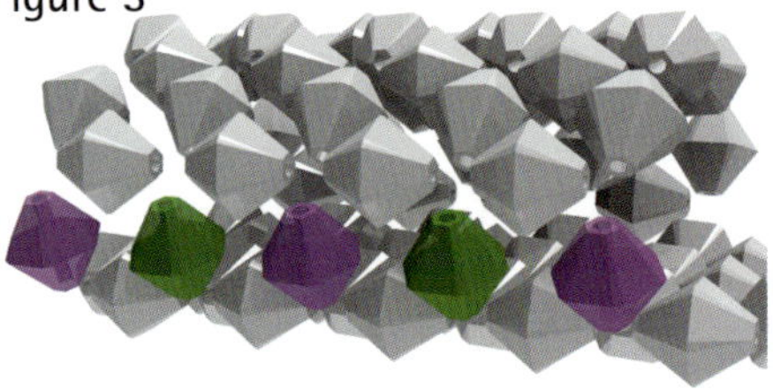

Figure 4

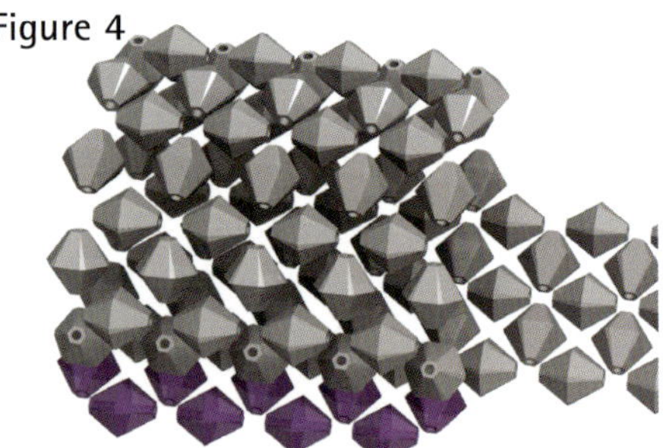

Obi, figure 1
Work the Obi in RAW (see page 94) using 2.5 mm bicones. First make a strip 2 units wide and 17 units long. Follow the chart for color placement.

Figure 2
Working from one edge, make another strip 4 units wide and 5 units long. Follow the chart for color placement.

Figure 3
Fold over the new strip and connect it to the lower edge.

Figure 4
Add one row of purple bicones to the lower edge of the long strip.

Attaching the obi
Bring the obi around the body and join the two ends of the long strip using RAW (this gives a total of 18 units).
With the obi in position around the body, exit one of the bicones along the top and then, using circular stitch, weave through one of the "up" Delica beads. Repeat all the way around the obi.

Emiko Variations

Turkish Delights

BEADS

4 g	11/0 Delica, #0312 Dark Raspberry
3 g	11/0 Delica, #1847 Sea Foam
2 g	11/0 Delica, #1841 Light Cranberry
2 g	11/0 Delica, #1835 Zest
2 g	11/0 Delica, #1838 Berry

OTHER

1	Needle case, 9 cm
12	Crystaletts, 3 mm, gold setting, Fuchsia
12	Crystaletts, 3 mm, gold setting, Sunflower
12	Crystaletts, 3 mm, gold setting, Sun

Brown acrylic paint

Base / Lid

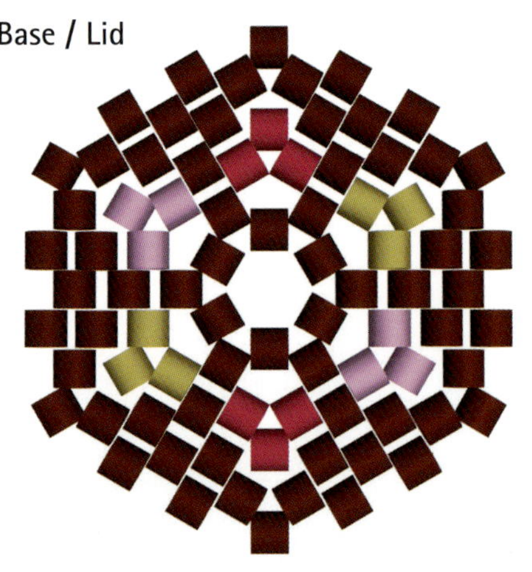

Base

Work the base following the figure on the left.

Body

Work the body from the bottom to the top following the chart. On the first round, add a Crystalett, for the second row just stitch through the existing Crystalett. The positions for the Crystallets are marked with white beads.

Lid

Work the lid following the figure on the left and the chart.

#1847
#1838
#1835
#1841
#0312

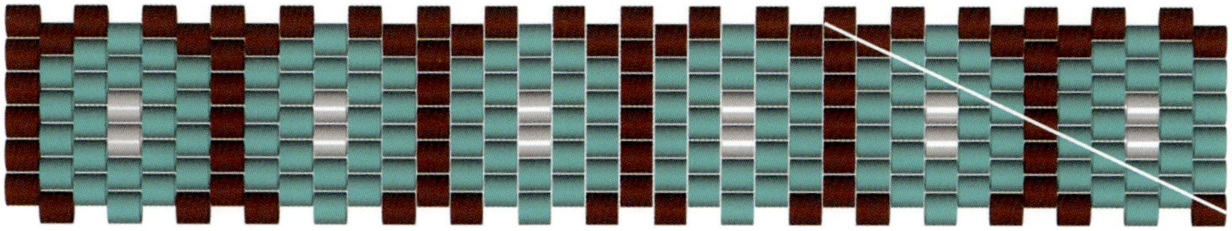

Leilani

BEADS

6 g	11/0 Delica, #0204 Medium Flesh (G)
1 g	11/0 Delica, #0923 Dark Purple
1 g	11/0 Delica, #0272 Goldenrod/Topaz
1 g	11/0 Delica, #0161 Orange
8	15/0 seed beads, #0595 Beige
2 g	11/0 seed beads, #0424 Burnt Orange (A)
1 g	11/0 seed beads, #0209 Fuchsia (B)
3.5 g	15/0 seed beads, #0411 Pea Green (C)
3.5 g	15/0 seed beads, #0416 Lime Green (D)
1 g	15/0 seed beads, #1310 Fuchsia (E)
1	8/0 seed bead, flesh color (neck)
1	Drop, 2.8 mm, #0401FR Black
1	O-Bead, Red Opaque AB

OTHER

1	Needle case, 6 cm
1	Polymer head bead "Leilani," 15 mm
12 cm	Jewelry wire
1	Metal bead, about 3 mm
1	Crimp bead

Flat-nose pliers

Awl

Base

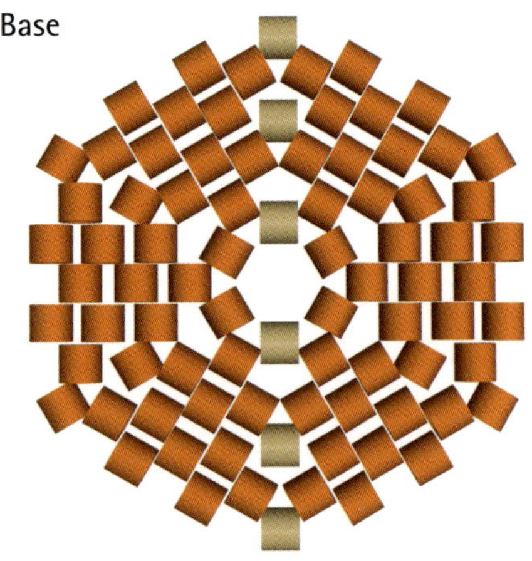

Lid

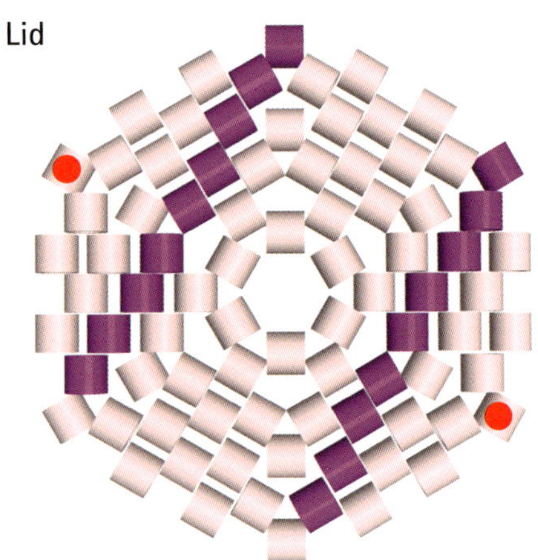

Base

Work the base following the figure on the left using Delica beads #0161 and #0272.

Body

Work the body from the bottom to the top following the chart.

Lid

Work the lid as shown in the figure on the left and the chart.
The red dots mark the position where you will later attach the arms.

Attaching the head

Make a hole in the center of the wooden lid with your awl. Fold the piece of jewelry wire in half, then thread on 1x drop. Thread both ends of the wire down through the head bead, pick up 1x 8/0 flesh-color seed bead, pass through the wooden lid, then add a 3 mm metal spacer bead and finally the crimp. Pull the wire down tightly, and at the same time push the crimp right up against the lid. You need to get it as tight as you can or the head will be wobbly. Using pliers, flatten the crimp. Then snip off the excess wire.
If your head spins too much, you can fix it in place with a little bit of glue on the inside of the lid - but if you do, make sure Leilani is looking in the right direction!

Skirt and arms

Explanation continues on page 44.

#0161
#0272
#0923
#0204

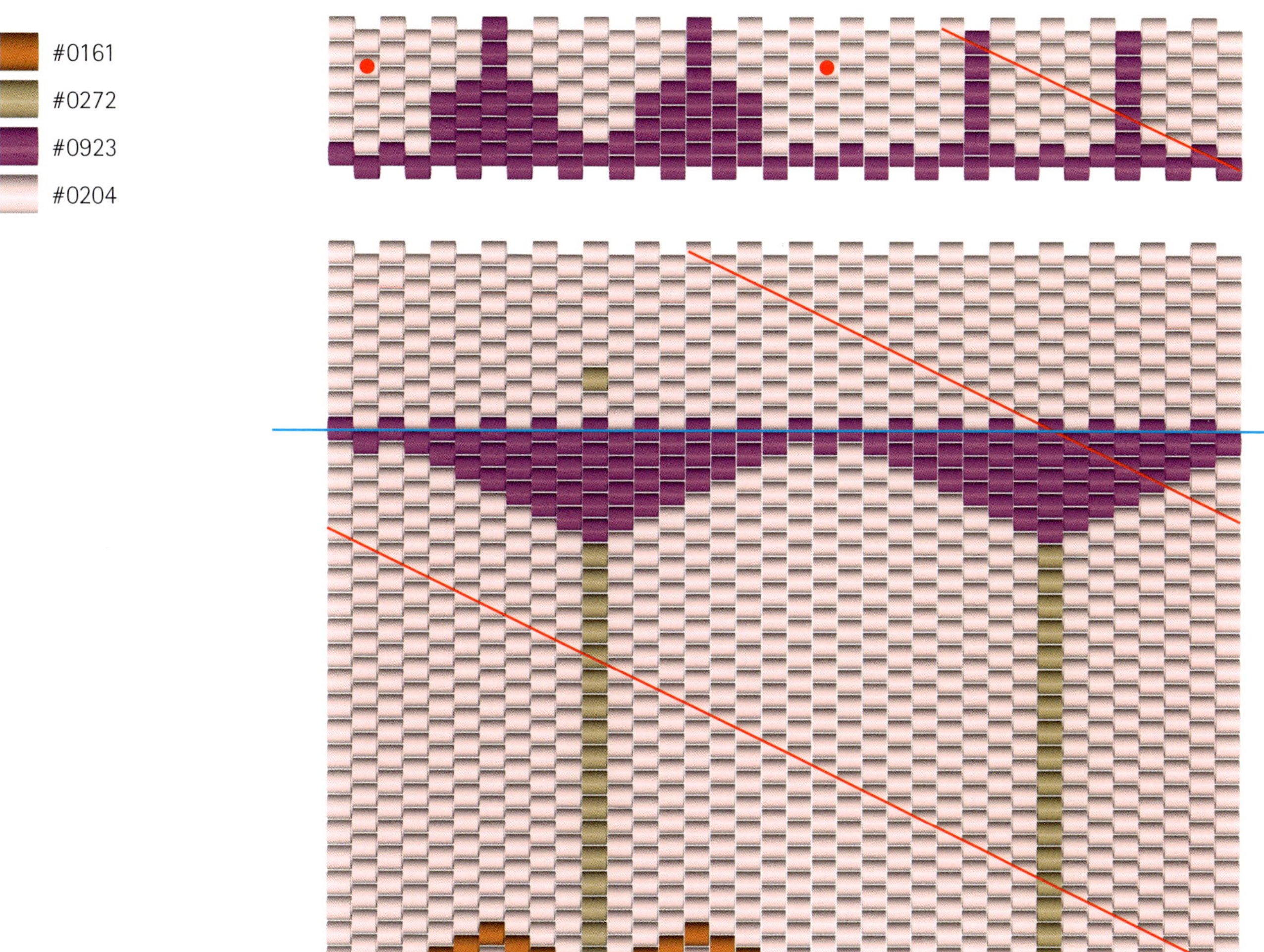

Figure 1

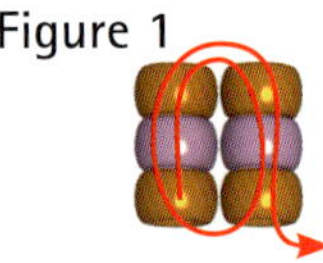

Figure 2

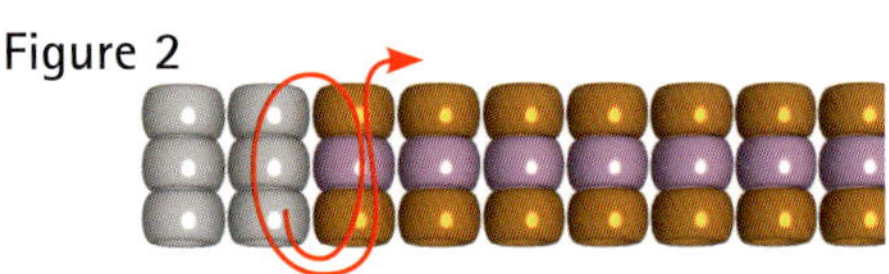

Figure 3

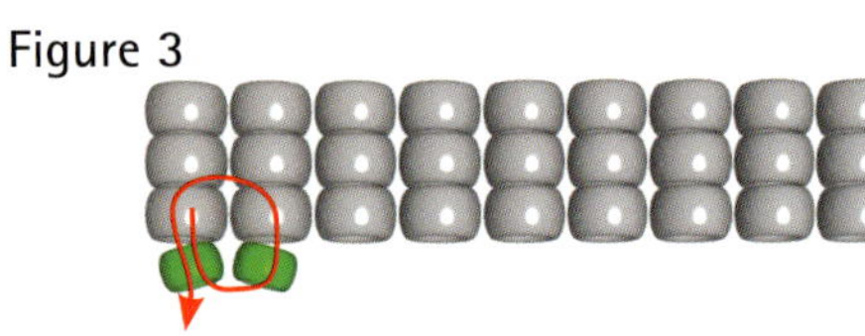

Figure 4

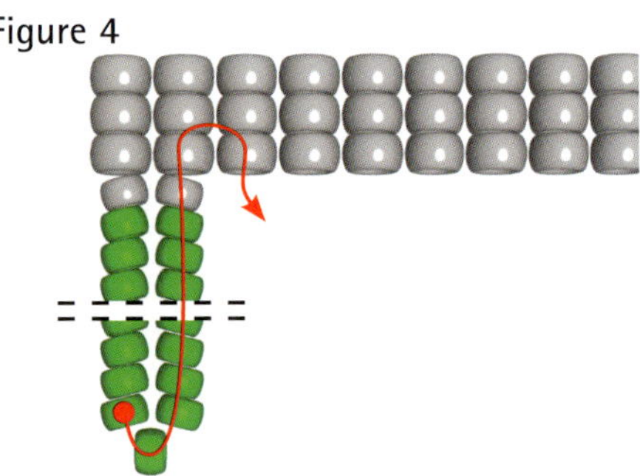

Figure 5

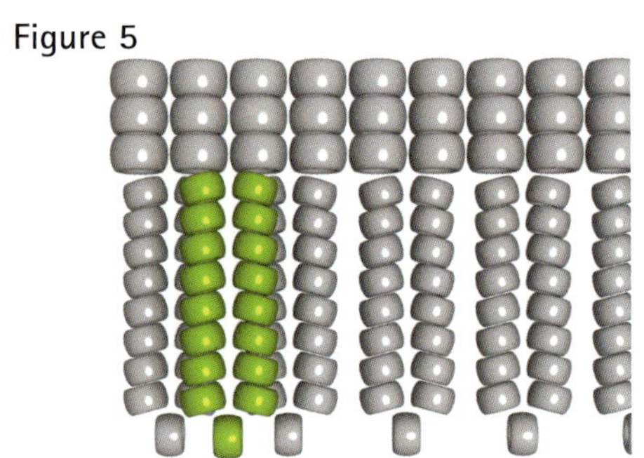

Skirt, figure 1

Pick up 1x 11/0 A, 1x 11/0 B, 2x 11/0 A, 1x 11/0 B and 1x 11/0 A seed bead and stitch through all the beads again. Arrange the beads so you have two stacks of three beads (ladder stitch).

Figure 2

Pick up 1x 11/0 A, 1x 11/0 B and 1x 11/0 A seed bead and stitch through the three last added and the three newly added beads. Repeat this until you have a strip of 28 groups of three beads. This is the waistband.

Figure 3

With your needle coming out of the last group of three beads, pick up 2x 15/0 C seed beads and stitch through the two lower beads of the last groups of three beads and on through the first 15/0 C seed bead just added.

Figure 4

From now on, always pick up 2x 15/0 C seed beads and stitch through the last two 15/0 C seed beads added (herringbone stitch). Repeat this until you have 28 pairs of seed beads.
For the turn, with your needle coming out of the bead marked with a red dot, pick up 1x 15/0 C seed bead and stitch up through the entire stack of 28 seed beads and on through the lower 11/0 seed beads of the waistband.
Repeat the steps for figures 3 and 4 all along the strip.

Figure 5

Add a second layer of strands on top of the first using 15/0 D seed beads. Stagger these strands so they fill the gaps of the first row; to achieve that, start from the second A bead.

Figure 6

Figure 7

Figure 8

Figure 6
Sew the skirt together at the seam and add a last stack of 15/0 D seed beads.

Figure 7
Slip the skirt over the body and sew it to Leilani's waist. To do this, with your needle coming out of an 11/0 A seed bead of the skirt, stitch through a Delica of the body and then through the next 11/0 seed bead of the skirt. Repeat this all the way around the body.

Flower, figure 8
Pick up 5x 15/0 A seed beads and weave through them again to make a ring. Pick up 7x 15/0 A and 1x 15/0 B seed bead, leave the last bead as a stopper and pass through the 7th bead. Pick up 5x 15/0 A seed beads, and pass through the first bead added after the circle then through the bead in the circle the thread is coming out of. Stitch forward through the next bead of the circle. Repeat this four more times.
Attach to the waistband of the skirt by using an O-Bead and 1x 11/0 seed bead as a stopper bead.

Figure 1

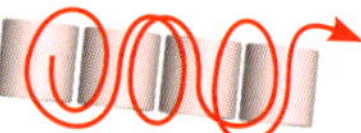

Figure 2

Figure 3

Figure 4

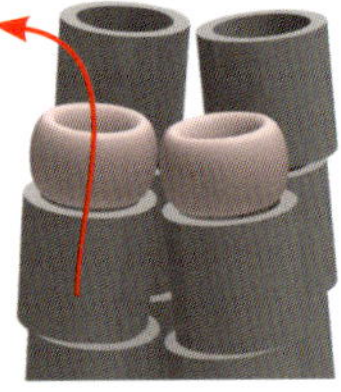

Figure 5

Arms, figure 1

Work the arms exclusively in skin-colored beads.
Stitch 4x 11/0 Delica together in ladder stitch (see also skirt, figure 1) and join them into a ring.

Figure 2

Pick up 2x 11/0 Delica and stitch down through the next Delica of the ring and up to the next (herringbone stitch).

Figure 3

Repeat the step for figure 2 and stitch up through the first Delica added in figure 2.
Repeat the steps for figures 2 and 3 until you have 10 Delica on top of each other.

Figure 4

Now you bead the elbow. To do this, just replace a pair of 11/0 Delica with a pair of 15/0 seed beads.
After this add 9 more rounds of 11/0 Delica.

Figure 5

Now you bead the thumb. Work this the same way as you worked before. To do so, pick up 2x 11/0 Delica and stitch through the beads below. Pick up 1x 15/0 seed bead and stitch through the beads so your needle is coming out of the bead marked red.
Note: Work the thumb on the same side as the elbow!

Figure 6

Figure 7

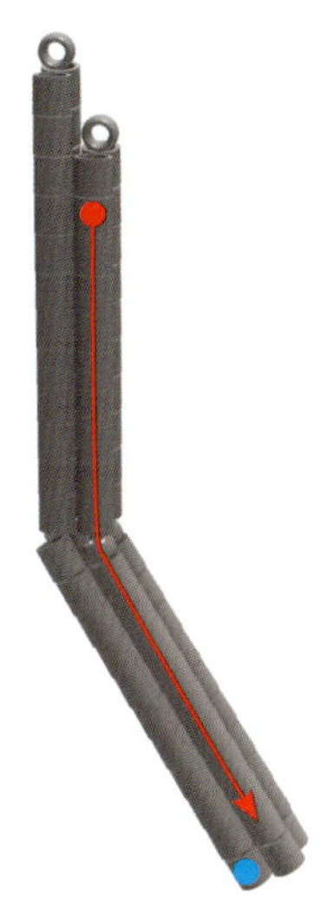

Figure 8

Figure 6
Add three pairs of 11/0 Delica as you did before and then work the fingertips like the thumb.

Figure 7
Weave through the beads so that your needle is coming out of the bead marked red. Stitch down through the stacks of beads, skipping the pair of 15/0 seed beads, then stitch up the adjacent stack, again skipping the 15/0 seed beads. Pull the thread gently, to create an elbow joint. At the end, stitch forward, so your needle is coming out of the bead marked blue.

Figure 8
For the shoulder, add 2 more rows on the same side as the hand.
Sew the beads marked red to the beads marked red on the lid (see pages 42 and 43).

Lighthouse

Materials

CRYSTALS FROM SWAROVSKI

1	Dome Bead (5541), 15 mm, Crystal AB
about 90	Flat Backs (2058), SS 10 in assorted colors: Aquamarine, Capri Blue, Sapphire, Light Sapphire
about 100	Flat Backs (2058), SS 10 in assorted colors: Crystal, Jet, Black Diamond

BEADS

3 g	11/0 Delica, #0774 Red
3 g	11/0 Delica, #0200 White
1 g	11/0 Delica, #0010 Black
36	11/0 Delica, #0721 Yellow
1	11/0 Delica, #0035 Silver
18	15/0 seed beads, #0401 Black
18	SuperDuo, Jet

OTHER

1	Needle case with cone, 6 cm
20 cm	Jewelry wire
2	Crimp beads
1	Metal spacer, about 3 mm
1	Crimp cover, 4 mm

Acrylic paint in gray and blue
Glue
Toothpick or cocktail stick
Pliers
Awl
Wire cutter

Top

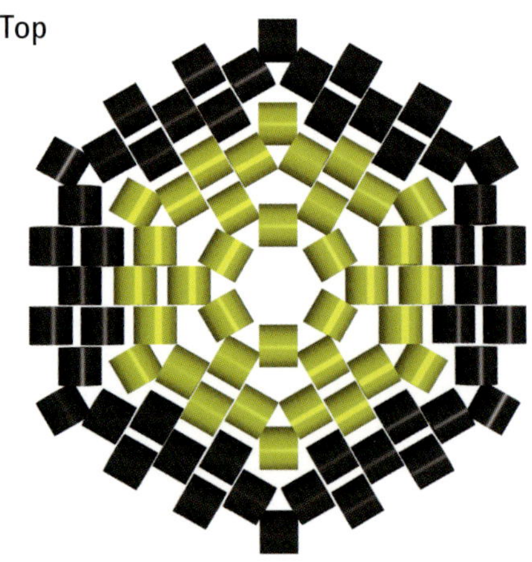

Figure 1

Base

Paint the cone two or three times with blue paint in the lower area (sea) and with gray paint in the upper area (rock). Let it dry.
Glue on the crystals as follows. There is no special pattern to do this, it's intuitive. Pick up a small amount of glue with your tooth-pick and dab it on to the base. Now put on the crystal and push it in place.
Hint: You may have a tendency to use too much glue. It would be a good idea to test it on a piece of paper a few times.

Body

First, make a hole in the center of the top of the case. You'll need this hole later for the dome bead.
Work the body from the bottom to the top following the chart.

Top

Work the top using Delica #0010 and #0721 following the figure and zip it to the body. Slip your work off the case for attaching the light (dome bead).
Fold the length of beading wire in half and poke the folded end down through the hole in the wooden case (you may find pliers helpful to do this). The two ends will still be poking out at the top, the folded end visible from the bottom. Thread a crimp bead onto the folded end (about a centimeter from the end) and flatten with pliers. Then pull on the two ends of the wire at the top so that the crimp bead disappears up inside the case and is right up inside the case as far as it will go. Then thread the two ends of the wire through your beaded body and as you do so position it back on the wooden case. Thread the dome bead onto the wire, then add a metal spacer bead and finally another crimp. Ensure you have a nice tight fit and then flatten the crimp with pliers and then cover the crimp with a crimp cover. Cut off the excess wire with wire cutters.
Hint: Doubling the wire ensures the crimp grips firmly; a single strand is not thick enough.

Bezel, figure 1

To make it easier to see, the newly added beads are shown in pink. Stitch 1x Delica #0010 in the ditch between the Delica of the light-house.

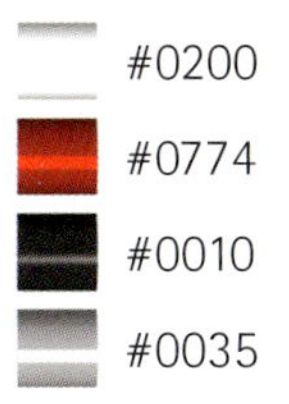

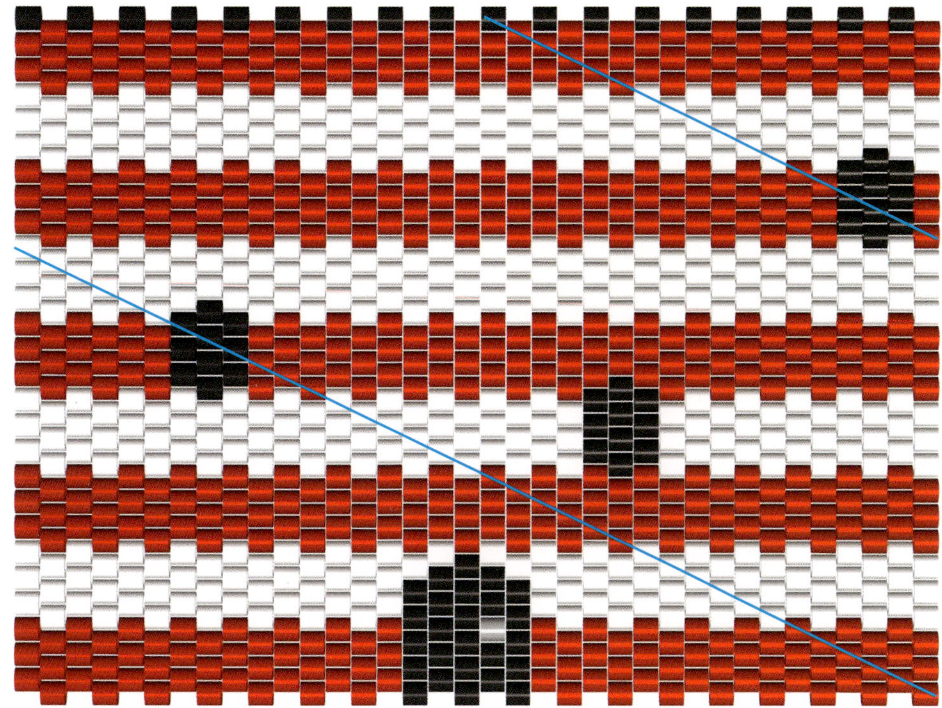

Figure 2

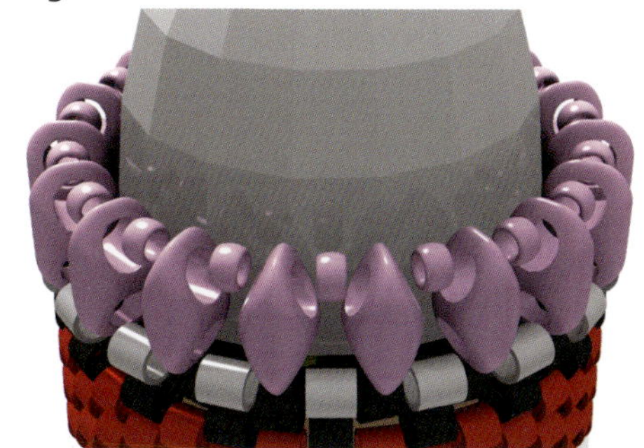

Figure 2

With your needle coming out of a Delica added in figure 1, * pick up 1x SuperDuo and stitch through the next Delica. Repeat from the * 17 more times. At the end stitch forward through the second hole of the SuperDuo.

Add 1x 15/0 seed bead between each SuperDuo. Sew in the thread and cut it off.

Zigzag

CRYSTALS FROM SWAROVSKI

1	Rivoli (1122), 14 mm, Coated Crystal Ultra Pink AB

BEADS

4 g	11/0 Delica, #0010 Black (A)
3 g	11/0 Delica, #2040 Mint Green
3 g	11/0 Delica, #2047 Orange (B)
3 g	11/0 Delica, #2035 Hot Pink (C)
1 g	15/0 seed beads, #0401 Black

OTHER

1	Needle case, 9 cm

Black acrylic paint

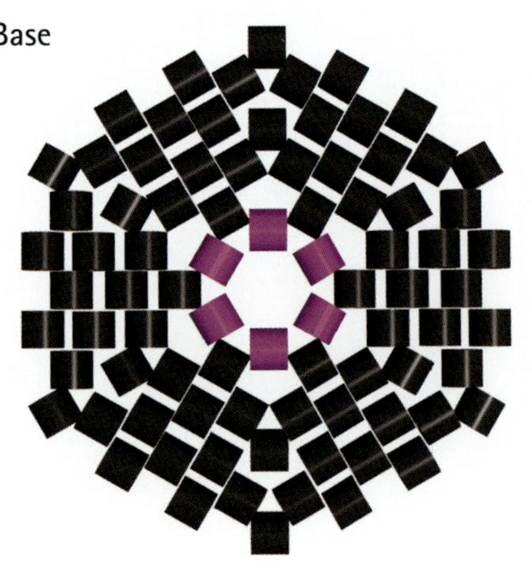

Base
Work the base following the pattern.

Body
Work the body following the chart on the right.

Lid
First work the body of the lid following the chart on the right. Then turn to the next page.

#2040
#2047
#2035
#0010

Figure 1

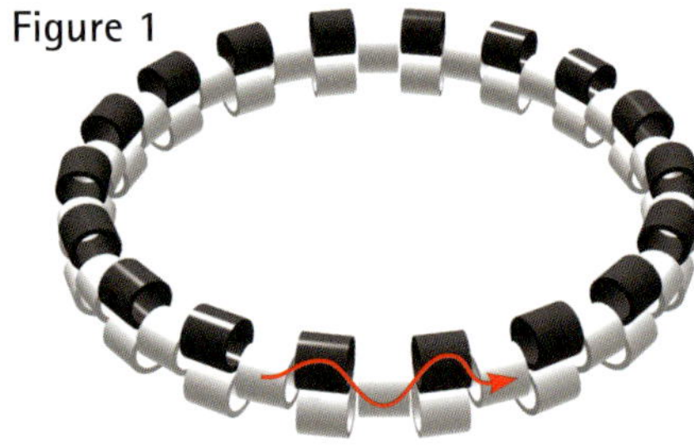

Figure 2

Figure 3

Figure 4

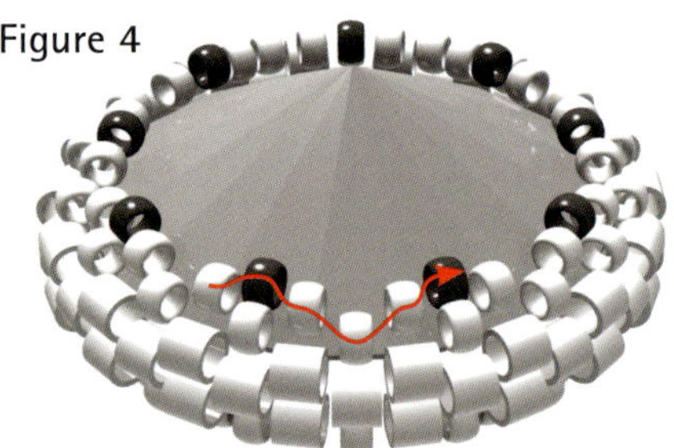

Lid, no diagram

Pick up 36x 11/0 A Delica, then tie the thread in a double knot to join the beads into a ring, leaving a tail about 20 cm long. Stitch forward through two Delica.

Figure 1

Add one round of 11/0 A Delica in peyote stitch. Work the step-up.

Figure 2

Add two rounds of 15/0 seed beads in peyote stitch. Work the step-up after each round.

Figure 3

Flip your work and put the rivoli face up into the bezel. Add two more rounds of 15/0 seed beads and work the step-up after each round.

Figure 4

Work another round of 15/0 seed beads, but this time add a bead only in every other gap, stitching through the beads of previous rows. At the end, stitch through the beads so that your needle is coming out of an 11/0 Delica in the middle round of the bezel.

Figure 5

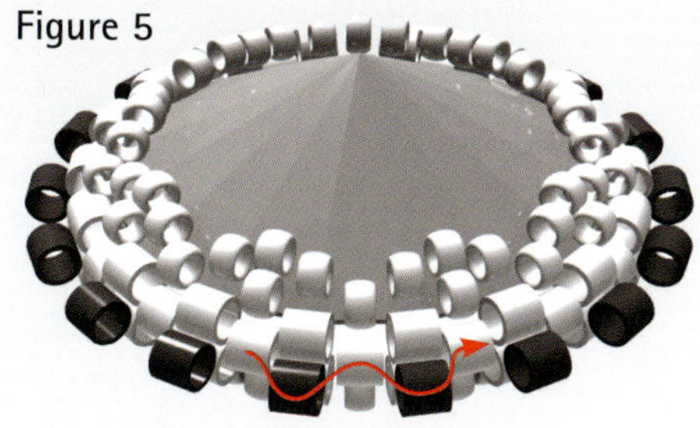

Figure 6

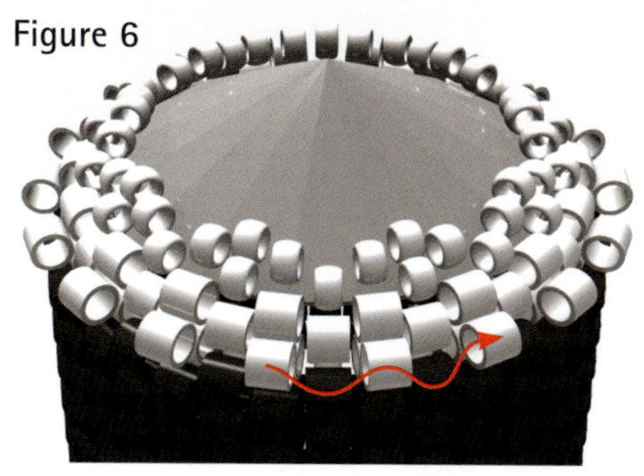

Figure 7

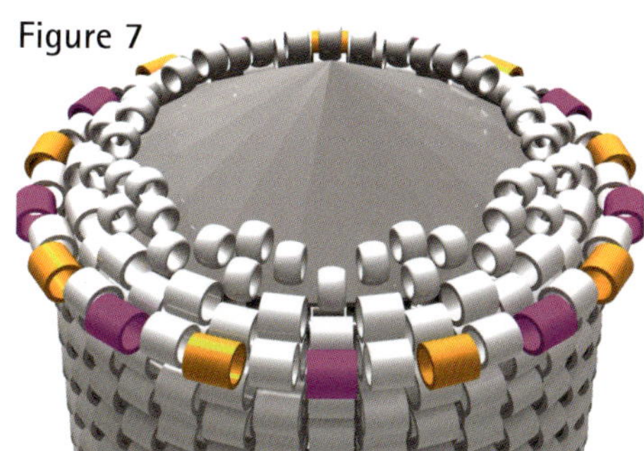

Figure 5
Add a 11/0 A Delica in every gap ("stitch in the ditch").

Figure 6
Now you need to check the sizing. Because the rivoli has a pointed back, there needs to be enough space to allow it to fit on top of the lid. You may need to add another row or two of 11/0 Delica to the lid section. When you have a nice fit, zip the bezel to the lid.

Figure 7
Weave back to the beads of figure 5 and add another round by "stitching in the ditch." Alternate between 11/0 B and 11/0 C Delica. Sew in the thread and cut it off.

Darcey

BEADS

3 g	11/0 Delica, #0626 Light Aqua
3 g	11/0 Delica, #0200 White
2 g	11/0 Delica, #1844 Dark Mint Green
2 g	11/0 Delica, #0353 Antique Beige
1 g	11/0 Delica, #0357 Pale Blue Gray
1 g	11/0 Delica, #0031 Gold
1	8/0 seed bead, flesh color (for the neck)
10 g	11/0 seed beads, #0571 Light Aqua
2 g	11/0 seed beads, #0131FR Crystal
17	11/0 seed beads, #4203 Yellow Gold
1	11/0 seed bead (or drop 3.4 mm), same color as hair
10 g	Drops, 3.4 mm, #0131FR Crystal
6	15/0 seed beads, #2022 Flesh

OTHER

1	Needle case, 6 cm
1	Polymer head bead "Darcey," 15 mm
12 cm	Jewelry wire
1	Crimp bead

Nylon thread, 0.25 mm, transparent
White acrylic paint
Awl
Pliers
Wire cutter

Lid

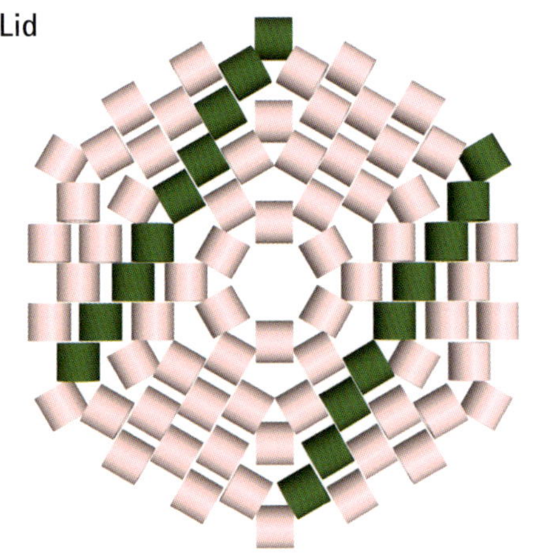

Figure 1

Figure 2

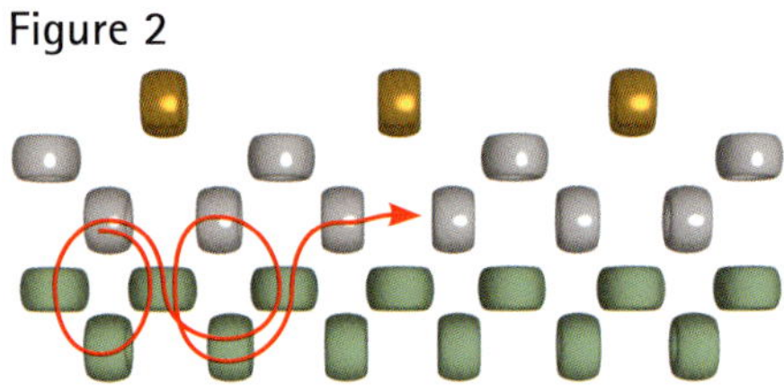

Base
Work the base using Delica #0200.

Body
Work the body following the chart on the right.

Lid
Work the lid as shown in the figure on the left and the chart.

Tutu (skirt)
"Stitch in the ditch", adding 1x 11/0 gold seed bead in each gap. The pink line in the chart shows the position.
Important: Change to nylon thread; this is crucial to achieve a really frilly and stiff tutu.

Figure 1
This is the first increase round; if nothing else is mentioned, work with 11/0 #0571 seed beads. With your needle coming out of a gold seed bead, pick up 4x 11/0 seed beads and stitch through the bead out of which the thread is exiting and forward through the first bead added (right-angle weave, see page 94). Pick up 3x 11/0 seed beads and stitch through the next gold seed bead, the bead the thread is coming out of, and the next three 11/0 seed beads. Repeat this all the way around. When you get to the end of the round, join your last unit to the first (see also page 92, figure 2).

Figure 2
Work a normal round of RAW, but make sure you work a unit from each of the pair of beads. This will double the number of units that you worked in figure 1.

No figure

3rd round: Work another increase round as you did in figure 1.
4th round: Repeat the steps for figure 2.
5th round: Repeat the steps for figure 1 but replace the pair of 11/0 seed beads with 2x drop beads and use #0131FR as the "side" beads. This will create a nice frilly edge.

Attaching the head and the arms
Attach the head as you did with Leilani on page 42. Work the arms as described for Leilani on pages 46 to 47. Sew the hands together over her head.

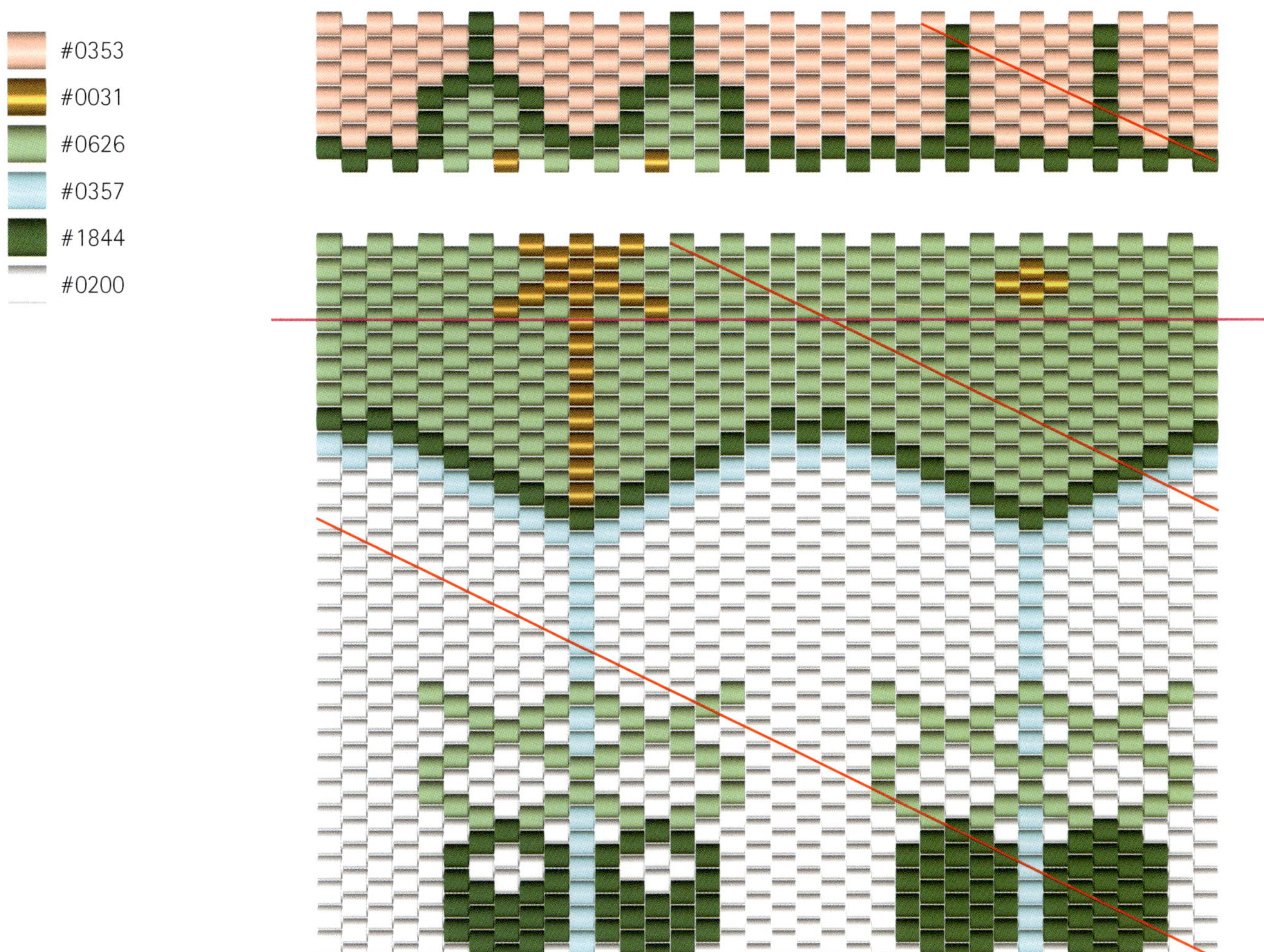
#0353
#0031
#0626
#0357
#1844
#0200

Perfume Bottle

Mauve Bottle

CRYSTALS FROM SWAROVSKI

1	Drop (6000), 28x14 mm, Crystal AB
12	Bicones (5328), 3 mm, Crystal AB 2x

BEADS

3 g	11/0 Delica, #0629 Lavender
2 g	11/0 Delica, #1831 Silver
1 g	11/0 Delica, #0670 White
10 g	11/0 seed beads, #0574 Lavender
1 g	11/0 seed beads, #0250 Crystal
5 g	15/0 seed beads, #0574 Lavender
2 g	15/0 seed beads, #0250 Crystal
1 g	15/0 seed beads, #4201 Silver
42	Round beads, 2 mm, White
1	Polaris bead, 10 mm, White

OTHER

1	Needle case with spherical base, 6 cm
20 cm	Jewelry wire
1	Crimp bead

Matching beading thread (like K.O.)
Lilac acrylic paint
Awl
Pliers
Wire cutter

White Bottle

CRYSTALS FROM SWAROVSKI

1	Drop (6000), 28x14 mm, Crystal AB
108	Bicones (5328), 3 mm, Crystal AB 2x
144	Bicones (5328), 4 mm, Crystal AB 2x
18	Round beads (5000), 2 mm, Crystal AB
12	Bicones (5328), 3 mm, Rose AB

BEADS

3 g	11/0 Delica, #0221 White
2 g	11/0 Delica, #1832 Gold
1 g	11/0 Delica, #0625 Pink
10 g	11/0 seed beads, #0551 White
1 g	11/0 seed beads, #0556 Pink
5 g	15/0 seed beads, #0551 White
2 g	15/0 seed beads, #0556 Pink
1 g	15/0 seed beads, #4202 Gold
42	Round beads, 2 mm, White Satin
1	Polaris bead, 10 mm, Pink

OTHER

1	Needle case with spherical base, 6 cm
20 cm	Jewelry wire
1	Crimp bead

Matching beading thread (like K.O.)
White acrylic paint
Awl
Pliers
Wire cutter
6lb Crystal FireLine

Figure 1

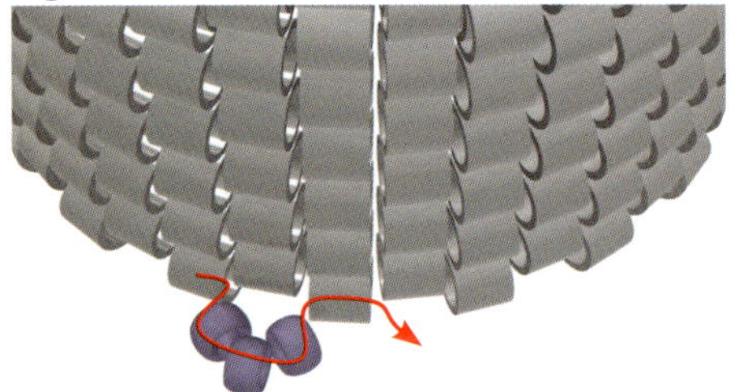

Figure 2

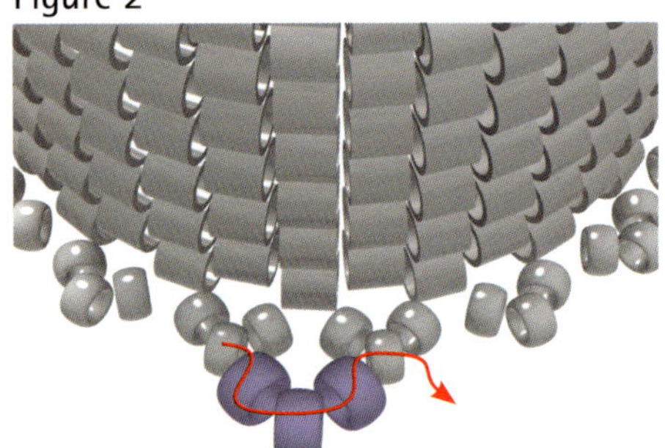

Note

Different bead colors/finishes can affect the outcome of this design. While working my samples, I discovered that the white beads were slightly smaller than the colored beads, and this made a huge difference in the overall size of the design. If you choose different beads from the ones suggested, you may have to alter the rows of netting.
I worked the base with a K.O. thread in a matching color.

Base for the mauve bottle

First paint your needle case with acrylic paint and allow it to dry. Because a lot of the needle case will be visible, this is an important step.
Start with the neck of the bottle and work in peyote for a total of 21 rounds with Delica.
Work one round of three-bead netting with 15/0 seed beads. To do so, pick up 3x 15/0 seed beads and stitch through the next Delica (figure 1). Repeat this all around the base.
With your needle coming out of the second 15/0 seed bead added, work 6 rounds of three-bead netting using 11/0 seed beads (figure 2).
Work 6 rounds of five-bead netting using 11/0 seed beads. To do so, just add 5x 11/0 seed beads instead of 3x 11/0 seed beads each time.
Work 3 rounds of three-bead netting using 11/0 seed beads, and repeat the last thread path to strengthen.
Note: Tight tension is required; pull your work in and down to cover the wooden form.

Base for the white bottle

First paint your needle case with acrylic paint and allow it to dry. Because a lot of the needle case will be visible, this is an important step.
Start with the neck of the bottle and work in peyote for a total of 21 rounds with Delica.
Work one round of three-bead netting with 15/0 seed beads. To do so, pick up 3x 15/0 seed beads and stitch through the next Delica (figure 1). Repeat this all around the base.
With your needle coming out of the second 15/0 seed bead added, work 5 rounds of three-bead netting using 11/0 seed beads (figure 2).
Work 8 rounds of five-bead netting using 11/0 seed beads. To do so, just add 5x 11/0 seed beads instead of 3x 11/0 seed beads each time.
Work 2 rounds of three-bead netting using 11/0 seed beads, and repeat the last thread path to strengthen.
Note: Tight tension is required; pull your work in and down to cover the wooden form.

Embellishing the white bottle

Switch to Fireline for adding the crystals.

Start at the top round, with your thread coming out of one of the vertical-holed 15/0 seed beads. Pick up 1x 15/0 seed bead, 1x 2-mm crystal bead and 1x 15/0 seed bead and pass through the next 15/0 seed bead. Repeat all the way around, then weave down to the next round.

Pick up 1x 15/0 seed bead, 1x 3-mm bicone and 1x 15/0 seed bead, then weave through the next horizontal bead. Repeat all the way around.

Work 3 more rounds using 3-mm bicones.

Work 8 rounds using 4-mm bicones.

Work 2 rounds using 3-mm bicones.

Note: If you decide to add crystals to the mauve bottle, you will need to adjust the number of rounds and size of crystals to fit your netting.

Figure 1

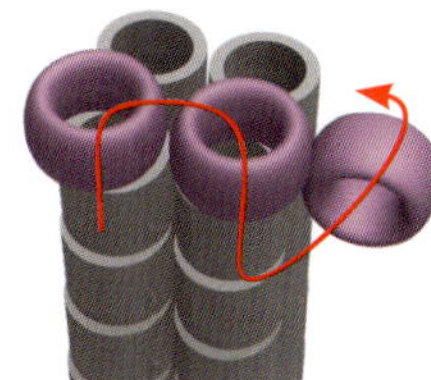

Figure 2

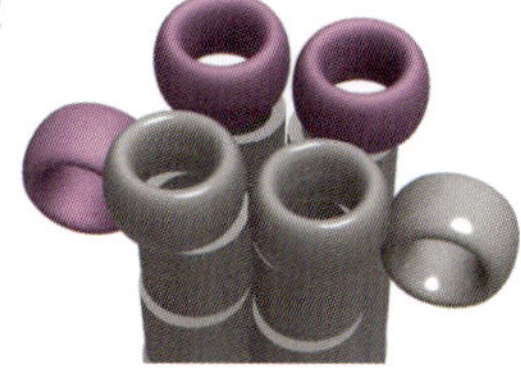

Cord (both bottles)

Work the cord as described for Leilani's arm on page 46. Start with a row of 4x Delica in ladder stitch and then work 32 rounds in herringbone stitch using Delica beads.

Figure 1

Pick up 2x 11/0 seed beads and weave down into the next stack as normal, pick up 1x 11/0 seed bead, then weave up one bead of the next stack.

Figure 2

Repeat the steps for figure 1.

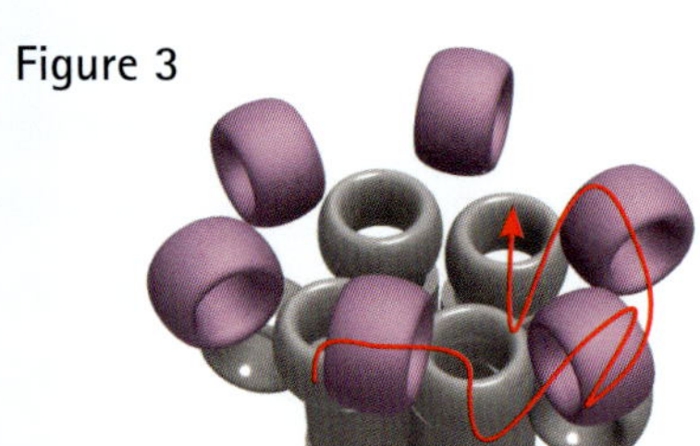

Figure 3

With your needle coming out of the first seed bead added in figure 1, pick up 1x 11/0 seed bead and weave down into the next stack, pick up 1x 11/0 seed bead, and pass through the 11/0 seed bead added in the previous round. Pick up 1x 11/0 seed bead and weave up through the next stack; repeat. This will give you 6 beads in the round.

No diagram

Work 5 rounds of three-bead netting as you did at the base; this will create a little "cup" shape to hold the Polaris bead.

Insert the Polaris bead into this cup, pick up 1x 11/0 seed bead, then stitch through the middle bead of the next three beads. Repeat all the way around, then repeat the thread path, pulling tight. If required, repeat the previous step.

Tassel (both bottles)

With your thread exiting one of the bottom 11/0 seed beads of the netted Polaris bead, pick up 30x 15/0 seed beads, 1x 11/0 Delica, 1x 3-mm bicone, 1x 11/0 Delica and 3x 15/0 seed beads. Leaving the last three 15/0 seed beads as stoppers, weave back up through all the other beads, then through the bead your thread was originally coming out of, but from the other side. Weave to the next 11/0 seed bead of the netting and repeat to do this all the way around.

Repeat the steps to make a second round of fringe.

Sew the finished tassel to the neck of the bottle.

Figure 1

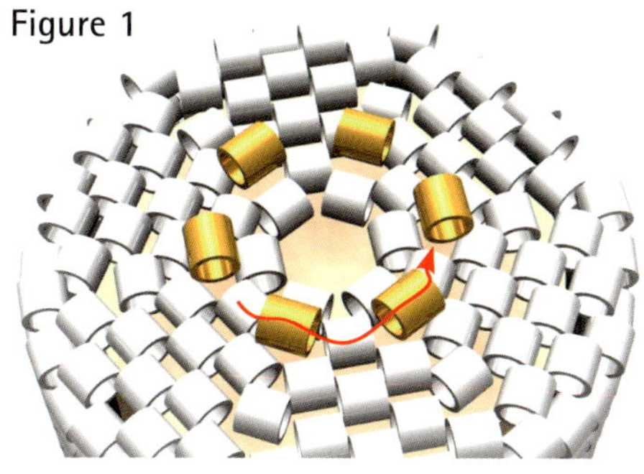

Figure 2

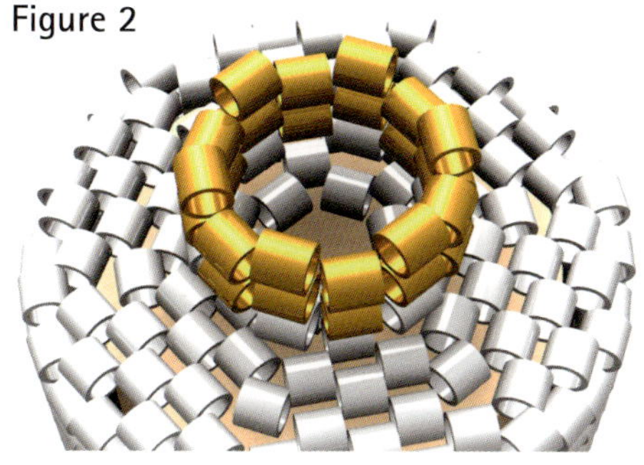

Figure 3

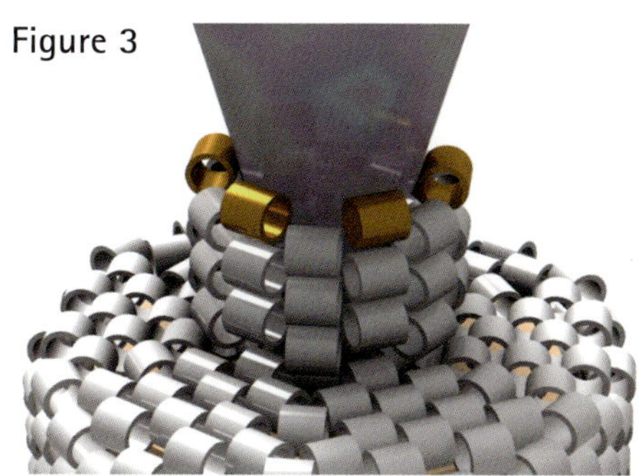

Lid (both bottles)
Work the lid as usual using Delica beads in gold or silver.

Figure 1
With your needle coming out of a Delica in the second round of the lid, pick up 1x 11/0 Delica and "stitch in the ditch" through the next Delica.

Figure 2
Add 3 more rounds in peyote, keeping a fairly tight tension; this is the "cup" to hold the crystal drop. Don't cut off your thread.

At this stage, you may wish to add a piece of double-sided tape to the wooden top to help keep your beadwork in position. With your beadwork in position, make a hole in the center of the wooden case using an awl.

Adding the big crystal drop
Fold the beading wire in half, then thread on the crystal drop. Thread both ends of the wire through your beaded cap and the wooden lid. Thread on a crimp and then, while pulling the wire tight and with the crystal drop in the correct upright position, flatten the crimp right up against the wooden case. If you wish, add a second crimp for security, then snip the excess wire.

Figure 3
Add another round in peyote, keeping a tight tension; repeat the thread path to strengthen the beadwork.

Figure 4

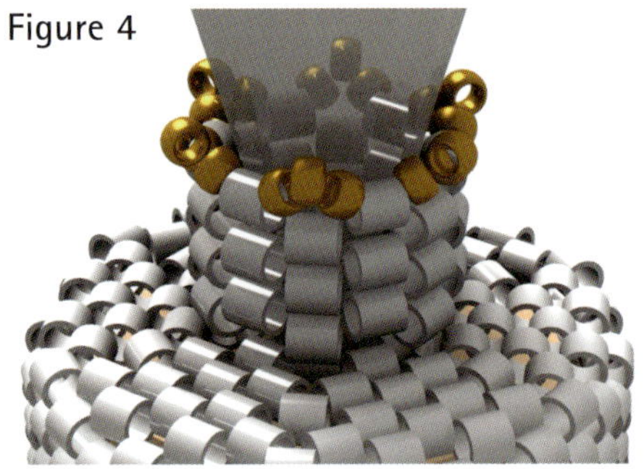

Figure 5

Figure 4
Add one more round in peyote stitch, this time adding 3x 15/0 seed beads in each gap. This will make little picots; don't step up at the end of the round.

Figure 5
Repeat the thread path of the last round, but this time use round 2-mm beads; these should sit in front of the picots. Repeat the thread path for strength.

Figure 6
Weave down to the first peyote round (figure 1). Pick up 4x 15/0 seed beads and stitch through the next Delica of the round. Repeat all the way around.

Figure 7
Weave forward through the first two beads added in figure 6, pick up 1x 15/0 seed bead and stitch forward to the middle of the next group of four beads. Repeat all the way around.

Figure 6

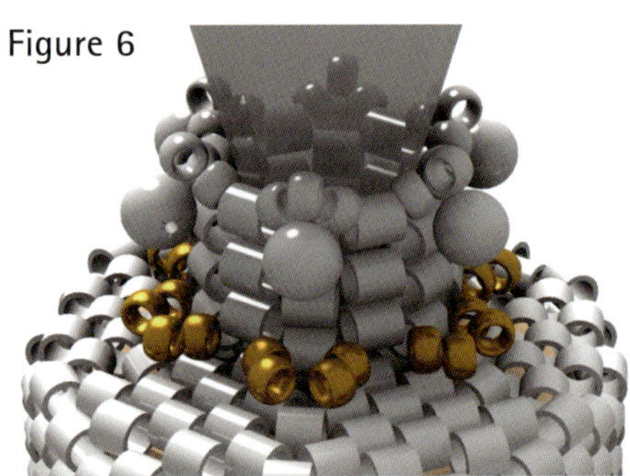

Figure 7

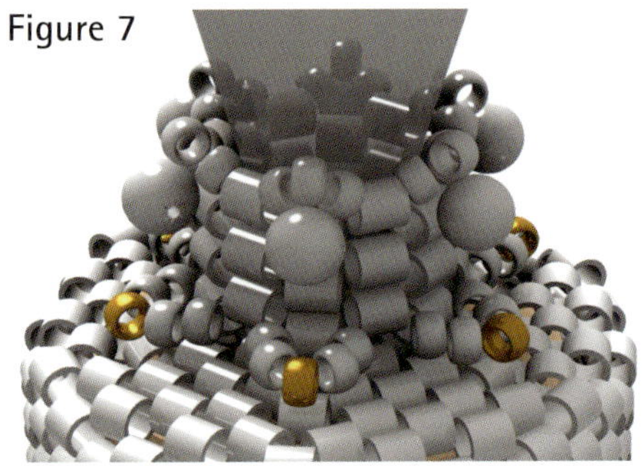

Figure 8

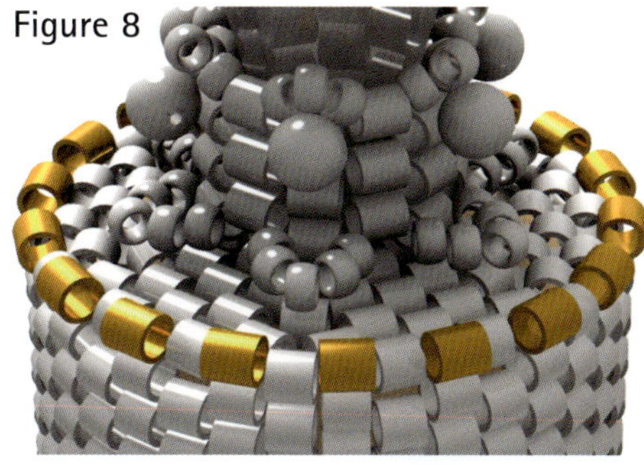

Figure 9

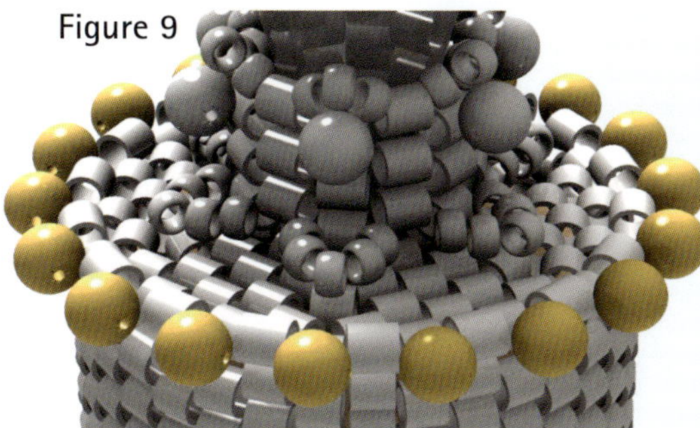

Figure 10

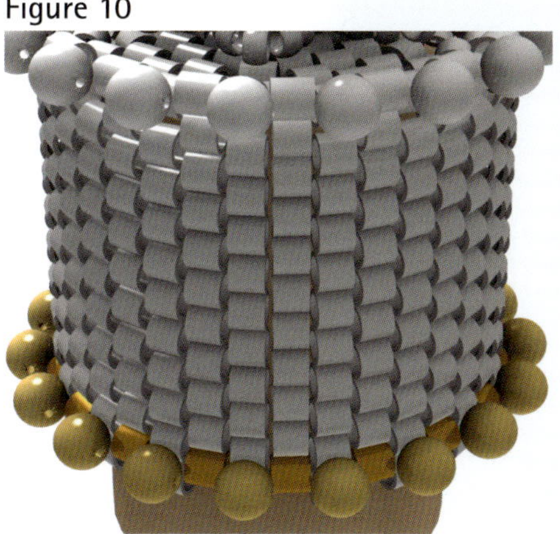

Figure 8

Weave your thread to the outside edge of the lid; this will be at the join where you zipped the two pieces together. "Stitch in the ditch," adding 1x 11/0 Delica in each gap. At the end, step up through the first bead added.

Figure 9

Add 1x round 2-mm bead in each gap.

Figure 10

Repeat the steps for figure 8 and 9 on the second round of peyote of the lid.

Hula Hoop

Needle Case

CRYSTALS FROM SWAROVSKI

72 Crystal Pearls (5810), 3 mm, Mystic Black
72 Round beads (5000), 2 mm, Jet

BEADS

6 g 11/0 Delica, #0010 Black
2 g 11/0 Delica, #0200 White
1 g 15/0 seed beads, #0401 Black
54 8/0 seed beads, #0401 Black
1 Spike, 12 x 18 mm, Jet

OTHER

1 Needle case, 6 cm
Black acrylic paint
Glue, double-sided tape

Rings

CRYSTALS FROM SWAROVSKI

69 Bicones (5328), 3 mm
2x 46 Round beads (5000), 2 mm

BEADS

Small amounts of each:
11/0 seed beads, different colors for each ring (here #0404, #0406, #0413, #0416, #1310)
15/0 seed beads, matching or contrasting for each ring
Selection of feature beads like Rizo, Mini-Drops 2.8 mm

Base
Work the base using Delica #0010.

Body
Work the body following the chart on the right.

Lid
Glue the spike bead on top of the wooden case and allow to dry completely.
Work the lid section and then attach it to the wooden lid with with double-sided tape. Complete the bezel around the spike. To do so, change to 15/0 seed beads and complete 4 more rounds of peyote, pulling in your work gently to capture the spike. Finally, add 1 round but add 1x 15/0 seed bead in every other gap to give a picot-effect edging.

Figure 1

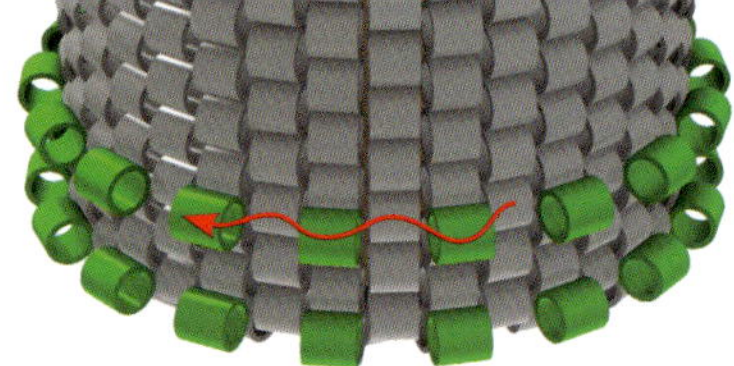

Bottom retaining section, figure 1
Referring to the pink lines in the chart for the body, "stitch in the ditch," adding 1x 11/0 Delica #0010 in each gap (2 rounds). These extra beads will be "top" and "bottom" beads for a round of right-angle weave (RAW, see also page 94).

Figure 2
With your needle coming out of one of the top Delica added in figure 1, work a round of RAW, *only* adding 8/0 seed beads.

Figure 2

#0200
#0010

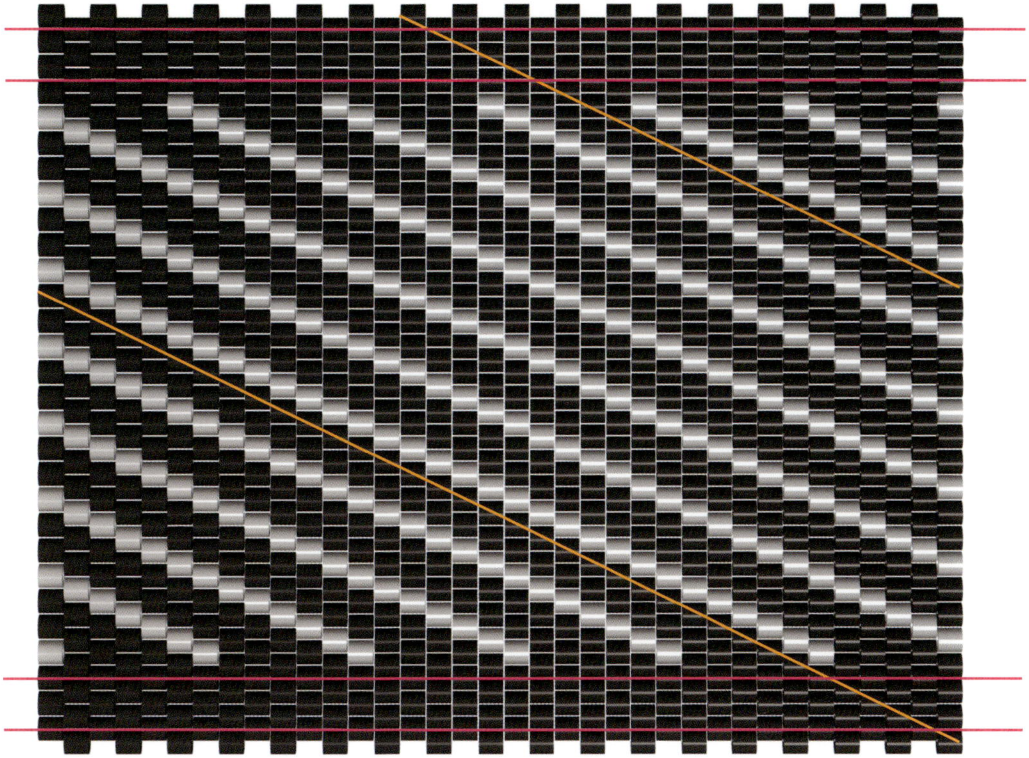

Figure 3

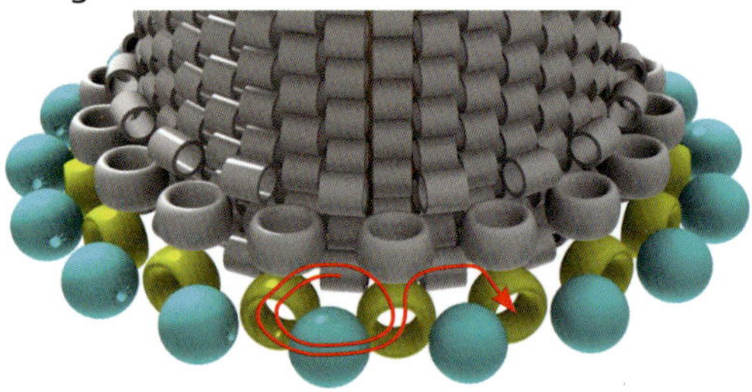

Figure 4

Figure 5

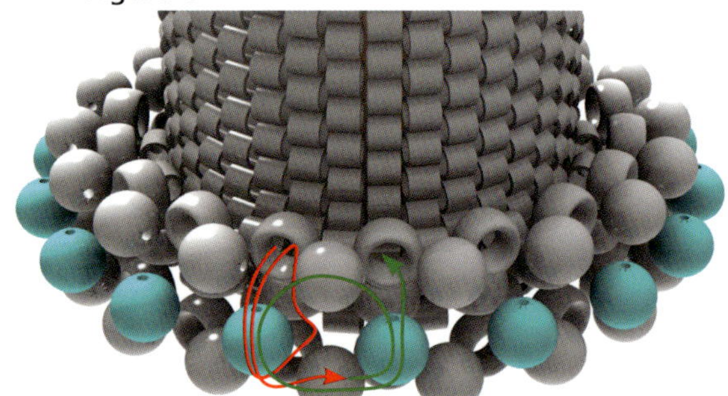

Figure 3
Using only the existing lower round of Delica added in figure 1, work another round of RAW, this time using 8/0 seed beads and Crystal Pearls.

Figure 4
Repeat the steps for figure 3 on the upper round of Delica added in figure 1.

Figure 5
Add a last round of Crystal Pearls as follows. With your needle exiting from an 8/0 seed bead added in figure 4, pick up 1x Crystal Pearl and stitch through the matching 8/0 seed bead from figure 3, the 8/0 seed bead of figure 2 and the 8/0 seed bead the thread is coming out of. Stitch forward through the just-added Crystal Pearl (red thread path).
Stitch through the Crystal Pearl added in figure 3, pick up 1x Crystal Pearl and stitch through the Crystal Pearl of figure 4 and the Crystal Pearl added before. Stitch forward through the next two Crystal Pearls and the 8/0 seed bead of figure 4.
Work around the needle case so every bead is connected.

Figure 6
With your needle coming out of a Crystal Pearl from figure 3, add 1x round 2-mm bead between each Crystal Pearl. Repeat this at the Crystal Pearls in figure 4.

Figure 6

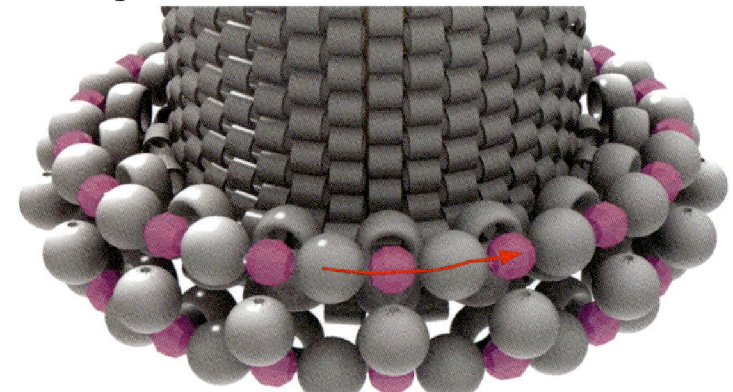

Now it's time for the rings

You can make as many (probably up to a maximum of 6) or as few rings as you like. My samples were made in cubic RAW (see page 96) using feature beads for effect. Play around with different beads to see what you come up with!

Ring 1

Ring 2

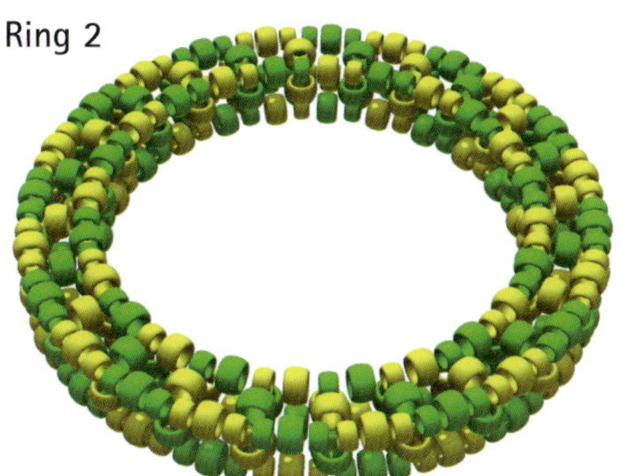

Ring 3

Ring 1 (orange on top)

Work 23 units in cubic RAW using 11/0 seed beads, and join them to make a ring (24 units total). Check the fit over the needle case; they should not be too tight so they can move and spin. Adjust the number of units if necessary by adding or removing beads. Stitch a 15/0 seed bead in between each 11/0 seed bead of the inner circle (2 rounds).

Stitch a round 2-mm crystal bead (5000) between each 11/0 seed bead of the outer circle (2 rounds). You can also try an 11/0 seed bead or a 2-mm fire-polished bead.

Ring 2

Work 24 units total using 11/0 seed beads. I embellished the inner and outer circle with 15/0 beads (1x in each gap in the inner and 2x in the outer circle).

Ring 3

This ring is also made of 24 units of 11/0 seed beads. In the base cubic RAW strip, I substituted a 2.8-mm Mini-Drop for every other bead of the outer edge. I embellished the inner and outer circle as in Ring 2.

<u>Note:</u> If you work with a tight tension, you may find that your ring is too small to fit over the beadwork; in that case, replace the 15/0 embellishment beads of the inner circle with size 11/0 seed beads.

Ring 4

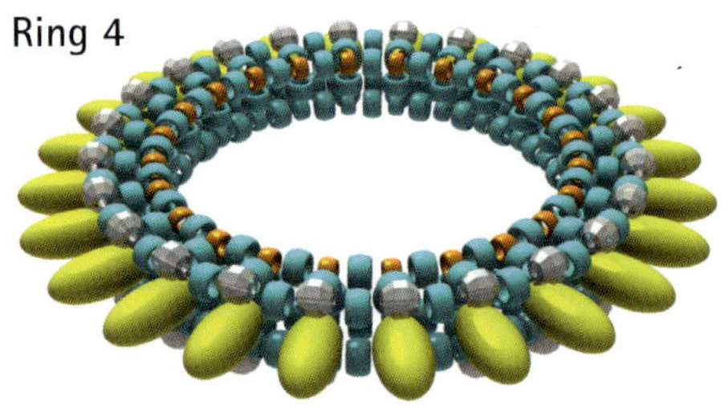

Ring 5

Ring 4

This ring is also made of 24 units total using 11/0 seed beads. In the base cubic RAW strip, I replaced every bead of the outer edge with a Rizo.

I embellished the inner circle with 15/0 seed beads and the outer circle with round 2-mm crystal beads.

Ring 5

This ring is made differently. First bead a flat RAW strip (see page 94) 23 units long using 11/0 seed beads. Join to make a ring (24 units total; the beads are colored gray in the figure). Check the fit of the ring.

Add the first side of 3-mm bicones in RAW (see thread path). Then add the third and last side, just adding 3-mm bicones. Embellish the inner circles with 1x 15/0 seed bead in each gap, and the outer circle (between the bicones) with 1x 15/0 seed bead in each gap (these beads are not shown in the diagram).

Top retaining section

Before you add the top retaining section, put your rings on your needle case.

Refer to the chart on page 73 for placement and "stitch in the ditch" to add 1x 11/0 Delica in each gap (2 rounds). These extra beads will be "top" and "bottom" beads for a round of RAW, as was done for the bottom retaining section.

Repeat the steps of figure 2 but use 3-mm crystal pearls. Then add a round 2-mm crystal bead (5000) between each gap of the Delica.

MATERIALS FOR THE NEEDLE CASE

CRYSTALS FROM SWAROVSKI

18	Crystal Pearls (5810), 3 mm, Bright Gold
54	Crystal Pearls (5810), 3 mm, Copper
36	Round beads (5000), 2 mm, Crystal Copper

BEADS

6 g	11/0 Delica, #1831 Silver
2 g	11/0 Delica, #1832 Gold
1 g	15/0 seed beads, #4202 Gold
54	8/0 seed beads, #4206 Muscat
1	Spike, 12 x 18 mm, Chalk Lila/Gold Luster

OTHER

1	Needle case, 6 cm

Gold acrylic paint, glue, double-sided tape

MATERIALS FOR THE RINGS

(4x Ring 5, 1x Ring 4)

CRYSTALS FROM SWAROVSKI

69	Bicones (5328), 3 mm, Rose Gold 2x
69	Bicones (5328), 3 mm, Aurum 2x
69	Bicones (5328), 3 mm, Crystal CAL 2x
69	Bicones (5328), 3 mm, Metallic Light Gold

BEADS

Small amounts of each in matching metallic colors:
11/0 and 15/0 seed beads (#4201, #4202, #4209, #4222)
Rizo

Skelly and Diva Skelly

Skelly

CRYSTALS FROM SWAROVSKI

1	Skull Bead (5750), 19 mm, Crystal Metallic Light Gold 2x
19	Bicones (5328), 4 mm, Chalk White
1	Bicone (5328), 3 mm, Chalk White

BEADS

6 g	11/0 Delica, #0310 Black
3 g	11/0 Delica, #0200 White
5 g	11/0 seed beads, #0402 White
1 g	15/0 seed beads, #0402 White
1	15/0 seed bead, #0401 Black
26	Bugle beads, 3 mm, #0402 White
10	Bugle beads, 6 mm, #0402 White
1	O-Bead, Jet

OTHER

1	Needle case, 6 cm
15 cm	Jewelry wire
1	Crimp bead
8	Closed jump rings, 3 mm
8	Eye pins, 5 cm
20	Head pins, 5 cm

Black acrylic paint
Awl
Pliers
Wire cutter

Diva Skelly

CRYSTALS FROM SWAROVSKI

1	Skull Bead (5750), 19 mm, Crystal Astral Pink
1	Bicone (5328), 3 mm, Crystal Astral Pink

BEADS

9 g	11/0 Delica, #0310 Black
3 g	11/0 Delica, #1840 Hot Pink
1 g	11/0 Delica, #0421 Burnt Orange
1	Rondelle with Crystals, 6 mm
1	Crystalett, 3 mm, silver setting, Crystal AB
1	Crown, 10 mm, Silver

OTHER

1	Needle case, 9 cm
15 cm	Jewelry wire
1	Crimp bead

Black acrylic paint
Awl
Pliers
Wire cutter

Base

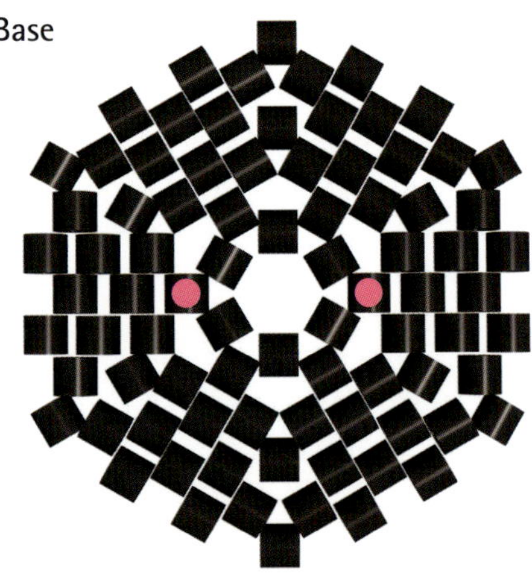

Lid

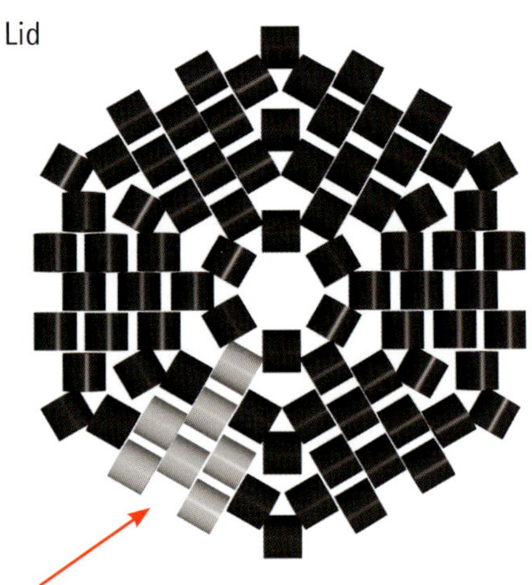

(For Diva Skelly, work the white beads in Hot Pink.)

SKELLY

Base
Work the base using Delica #0310.

Body
Work the body following the chart on the right.

Lid
Work the lid following the figure on the left and the chart, using Delica #0310 and #0200.

Attaching the skull
Use an awl to make a hole in the top of the wooden case.
Fold the beading wire in half, thread on 1x 15/0 seed bead (black) and position it at the fold, then pass both ends through the O-Bead, skull, 3-mm bicone, 4-mm bicone and wooden lid. Crimp into position, making sure you get a really tight fit.

Attaching the closed jump rings for arms and legs
Sew the closed jump rings to the beads marked with pink dots as shown in the diagrams of the base and the body.

DIVA SKELLY

Base
Work the base using Delica #0310.

Body
Work the body following the chart on page 83.

Lid
Work the lid following the figure on the left and the chart, using Delica #0310 and #1840.

Attaching the skull
Make a hole in the top of the wooden case with an awl.
Fold the beading wire in half, thread on 1x Crystalett and position it at the fold, then pass both ends through the crown, skull, 3-mm bicone, rondelle and wooden lid. Crimp into position.

#0200

#0310

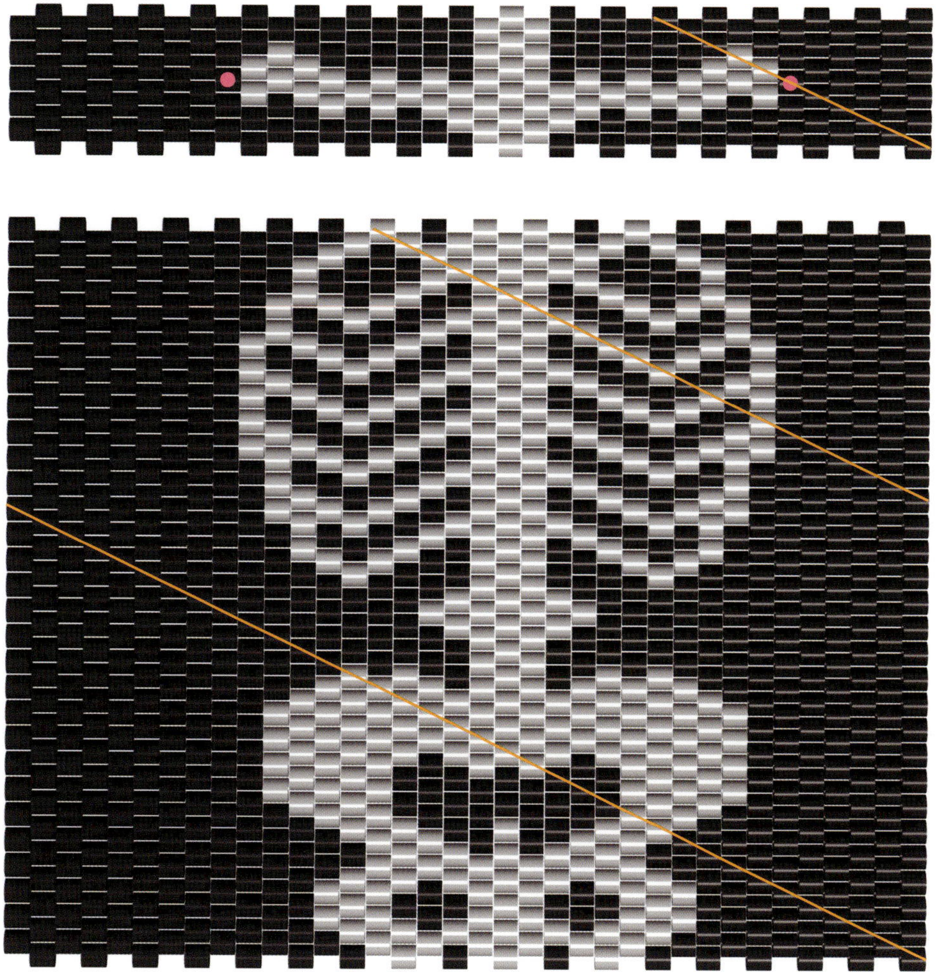

Figure 1

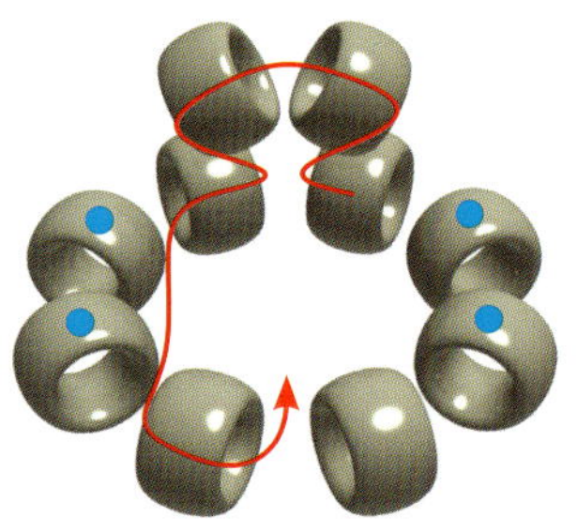

Arms and legs, no diagram

The arms and legs are made in tubular herringbone stitch. Start the herringbone tubes in the "traditional" way. This way works best because you can work from both ends of the tube.

Figure 1

Pick up 8x 11/0 seed beads and close them into a ring. * Pick up 2x 11/0 seed beads and stitch through the very next bead. Skip the next two beads in the circle and stitch through the next bead (figure 1). Repeat from * and step up through the first bead added in this step. Then continue in normal herringbone stitch.

Finish each end of the bone as follows. With your needle coming out of one of the top beads, pick up 1x 15/0 seed bead and weave down through the next two beads. Go up through two beads in the next stack, pick up 1x 15/0 seed bead, then weave down through the beads. Secure your threads and snip off.

Work these elements twice:

Upper arm: 14-bead stack; forearm: 12-bead stack; thigh bone: 16-bead stack; lower leg: 14-bead stack.

Assembling the arms

On an eye pin, pick up 1x 4-mm bicone, the upper arm and 1x 4-mm bicone. Snip off the excess wire and bend a loop (see page 97). Attach to the closed ring at one shoulder. Repeat a second time but attach to the other shoulder.

On an eye pin, pick up 1x 4-mm bicone, the forearm and 1x 4-mm bicone. Make a loop and attach to one upper arm. Repeat a second time but attach to the other upper arm.

On a head pin, pick up 1x 3-mm bugle bead, 1x 11/0 seed bead and 1x 3-mm bugle bead. Snip off the excess wire and bend a loop. Repeat 7 more times to make a total of 8 fingers. On a head pin, pick up 1x 3-mm bugle bead and make a loop. Repeat one more time to make a total of two thumbs.

Thread four fingers and one thumb on a closed jump ring and attach it to one of the forearms. Repeat for the other arm.

Assembling the legs

Assemble the legs as you did the arms. To make each of the eight toes, pick up 1x 3-mm bugle bead, 1x 11/0 seed bead and 1x 6-mm bugle bead on a head pin and bend a loop. For the two big toes, pick up 1x 6-mm bugle bead and bend a loop. Thread four of the toes and one big toe on a closed jump ring and attach it to one of the lower legs. Repeat once, but attach the toes to the other lower leg.

#0421

#1840

#0310

Nashville

Materials

BEADS

8 g	11/0 Delica, #1496 Pale Green
2 g	11/0 Delica, #0603 Ruby Red
1 g	11/0 Delica, #1202 Cherry Cola
1 g	11/0 Delica, #1831F Silver
1 g	11/0 Delica, #0010 Black
1 g	11/0 Delica, #0035 Silver
1 g	11/0 Delica, #0150 Brown
1 g	11/0 Delica, #0202 White
1 g	11/0 Delica, #0001 Hematite
4	Mini-Drops, 2.8 mm, #4201 Silver

OTHER

1	Needle case, 9 cm

Light green acrylic paint

Base
Work the base using Delica #1496.

Body
Work the body following the chart on the right. Instead of a Delica add a Mini-Drop at the green/white marked beads.

Lid
Work the lid using Delica #1496, following the chart.

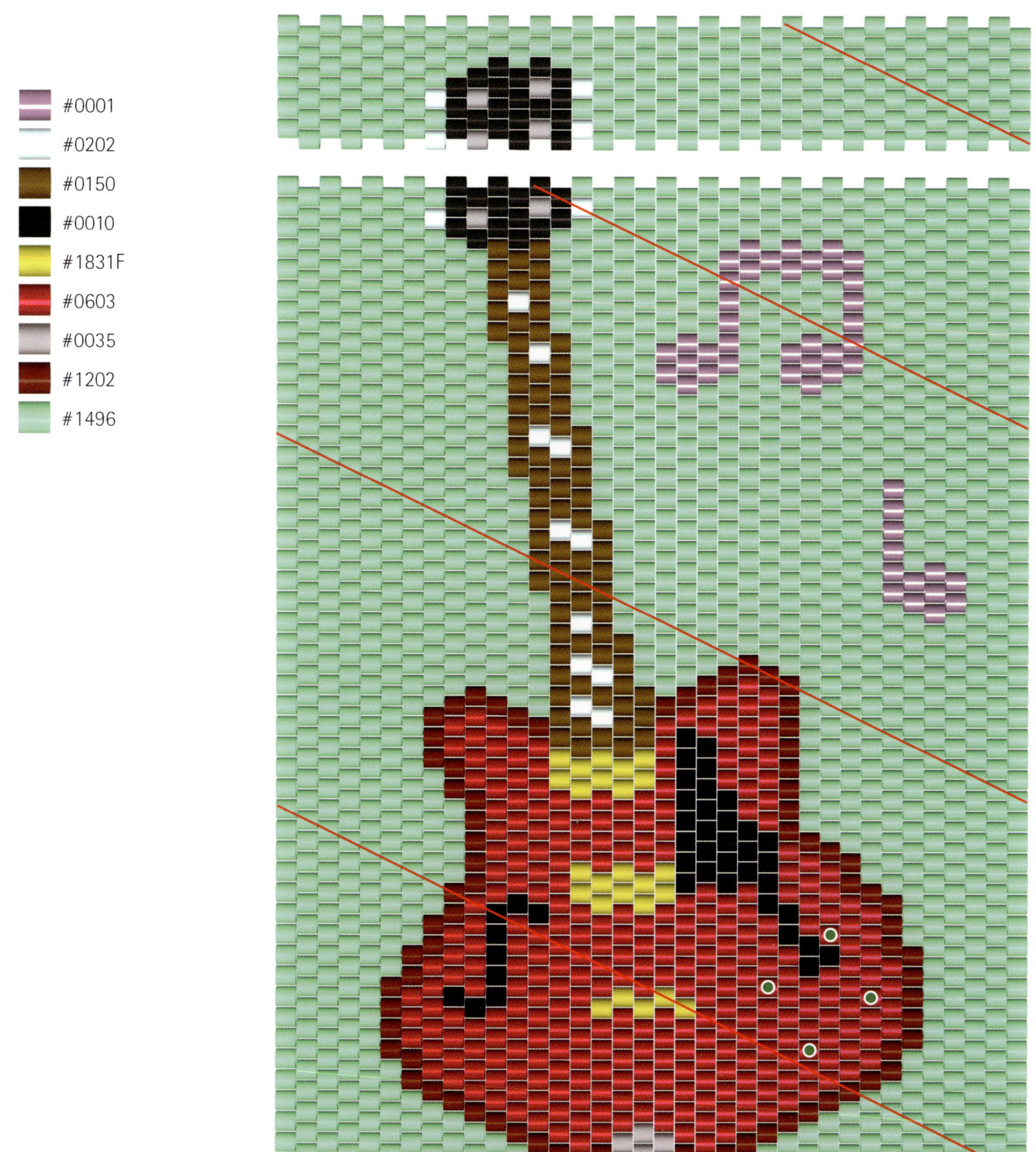
#0001
#0202
#0150
#0010
#1831F
#0603
#0035
#1202
#1496

Belle of the Ball

Materials

CRYSTALS FROM SWAROVSKI

36	Bicones (5328), 4 mm, Rose AB 2x
18	Round Crystal beads (5000), 2 mm, Rose (optional)

BEADS

5 g	11/0 Delica, #0353 Antique Beige
2 g	11/0 Delica, #0246 Hot Pink
1 g	11/0 Delica, #1840 Hot Pink
1 g	11/0 Delica, #0629 Lavender
1 g	11/0 Delica, #0208 Golden Oak
10 g	11/0 seed beads, #0643 Light Pink
1	8/0 seed bead, neck color
10 g	8/0 seed beads, #0355 Hot Pink
1	Drop, 2.8 mm, hair color
24	Round beads, 2 mm, Dark Pink
6	15/0 seed beads, #2022 flesh

OTHER

1	Needle case, 6 cm
1	Polymer head bead "Belle," 15 mm
12 cm	Jewelry wire
1	Crimp bead

Nylon thread, 0.25 mm, transparent
Awl
Pliers
Wire cutter

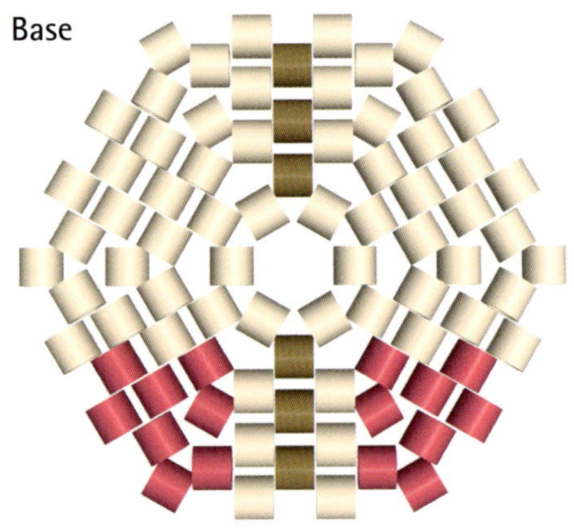

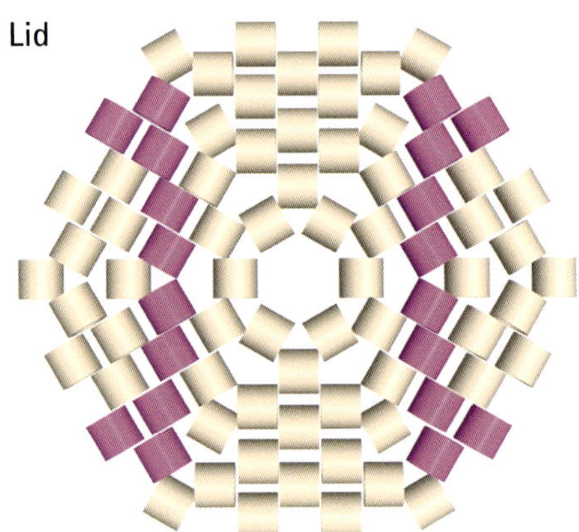

Base
Work the base as the diagram shows.

Body
Work the body following the chart on the right.

Lid
Work the lid as shown in the figure on the left and the chart.

Attaching the head
Before you attach the head, string on 15x 2-mm round beads and join them to make a ring for a necklace.
Attach the head as you did for Leilani, on page 42.

Arms
Work the arms as you did for Leilani on page 46. String on 9x 2-mm round beads and join them into a ring to make a bracelet. Sew in the thread and put the bracelet on her arm.
Sew the hands together.

The dress
See next pages.

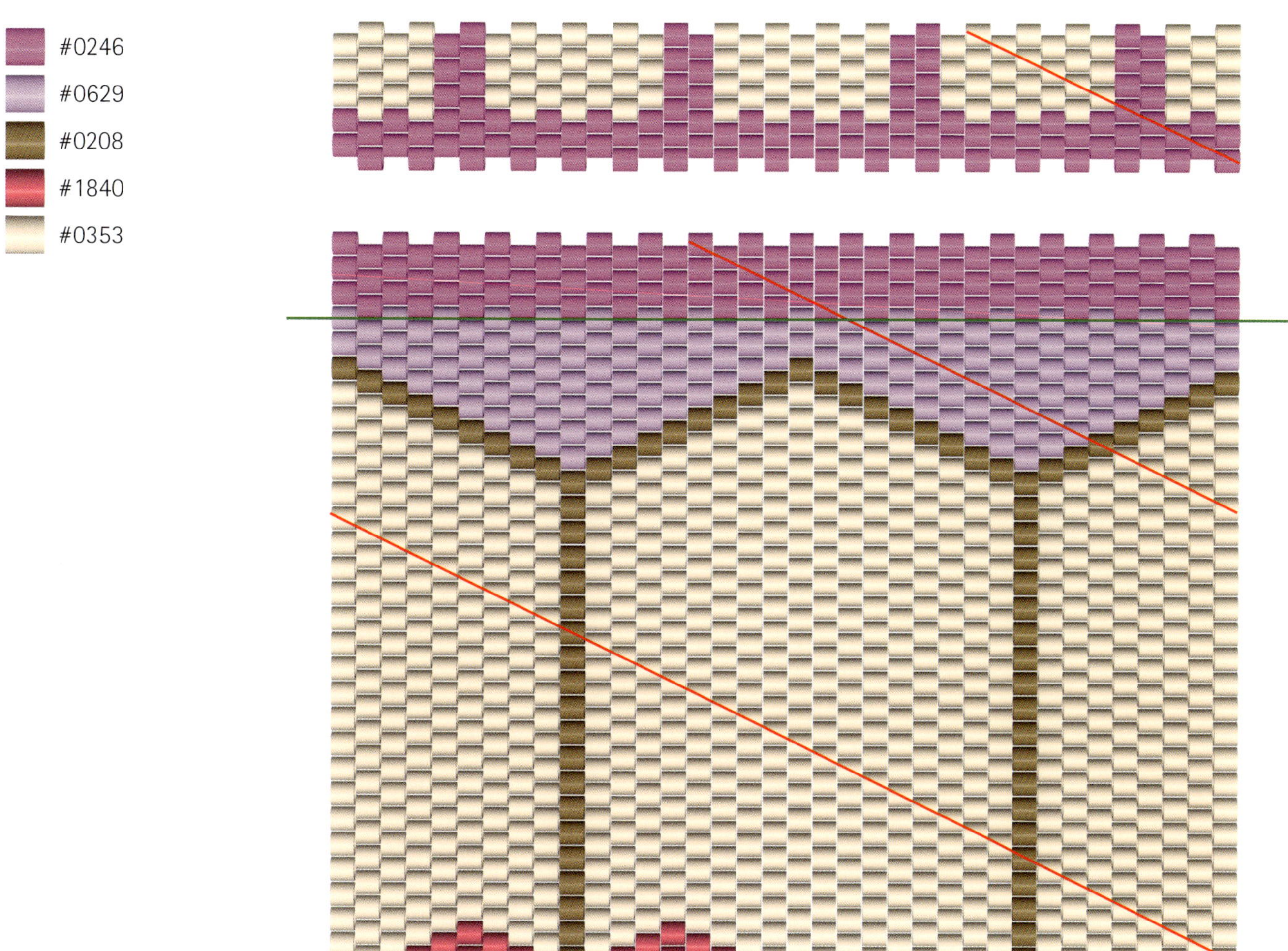
#0246
#0629
#0208
#1840
#0353

Figure 1

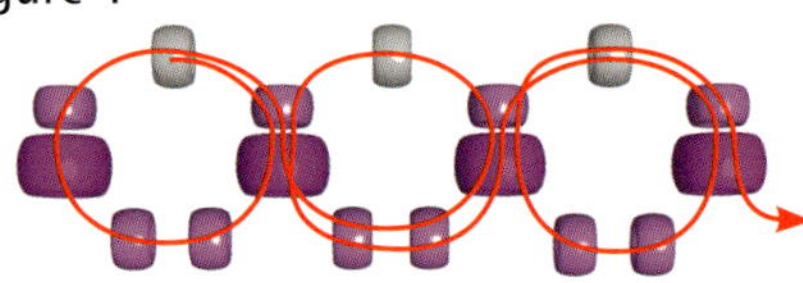

Figure 2

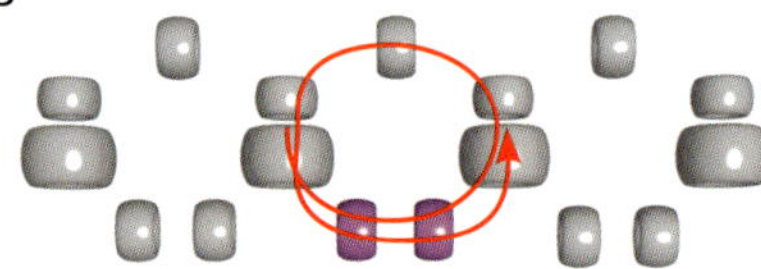

Figure 3

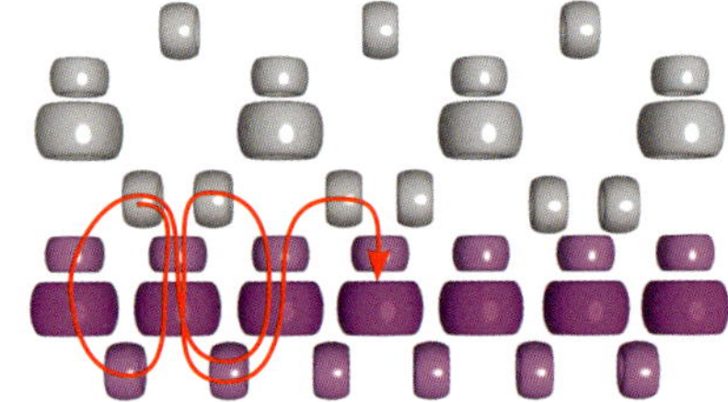

Figure 4

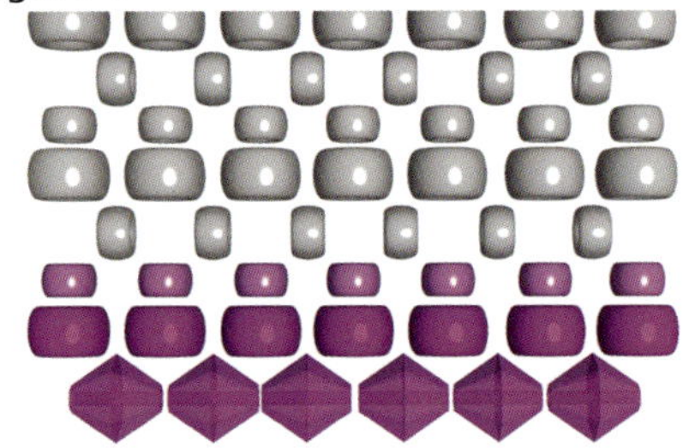

The dress

"Stitch in the ditch" to add 1x 11/0 seed bead in each gap along the line between the top and the underwear of the body (indicated with a green line on page 91). These newly added beads are shown in gray in figure 1.
Now switch to nylon thread to give the dress the right stiffness.

Figure 1

Pick up 1x 11/0, 1x 8/0, 2x 11/0, 1x 8/0 and 1x 11/0 seed bead, and stitch through the 11/0 bead out of which the thread is exiting and forward through the first 11/0 and 8/0 seed bead added. Pick up 2x 11/0, 1x 8/0 and 1x 11/0 bead, and stitch through the next "stitch in the ditch" 11/0 seed bead and forward through the 11/0, 8/0, two 11/0, 8/0, 11/0 and the next "stitch in the ditch" 11/0 seed bead. Pick up 1x 11/0, 1x 8/0 and 2x 11/0 seed beads and stitch forward until your needle comes out of the newly added 8/0 seed bead. Repeat this all the way around the body.

Figure 2

To complete the round just add 2x 11/0 seed beads as shown.

Figure 3

Add a second round and double the amount of units by adding a RAW unit at every 11/0 seed bead.
Then work another 8 rounds without increases.

Figure 4

Add a final round and replace the 11/0 seed at the bottom of the unit with a 4-mm bicone. This will give a nice ruffled edge.

No figure and optional

If you like, you can add some round 2-mm crystal beads between the 11/0 "stitch in the ditch" beads.

Right-Angle Weave

Figure 1

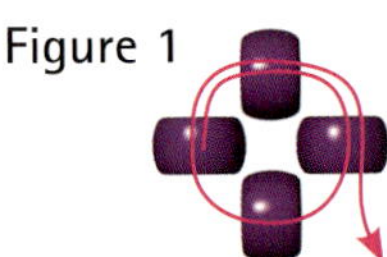

Figure 2

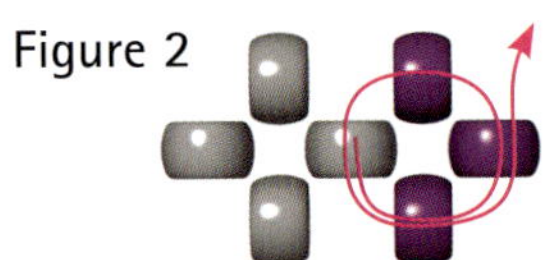

Figure 3

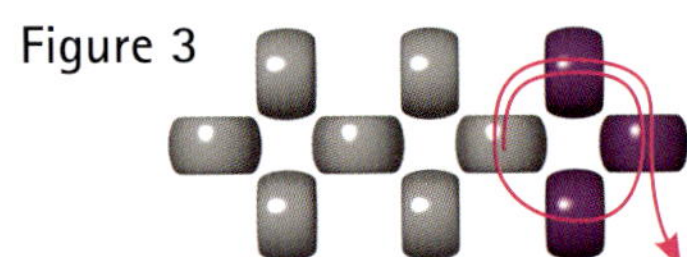

Figure 4

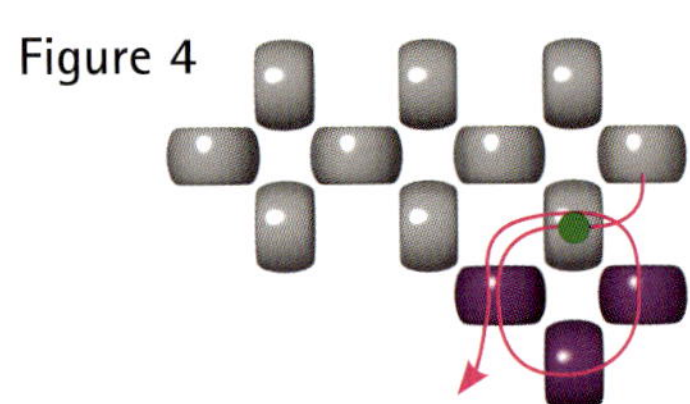

Figure 5

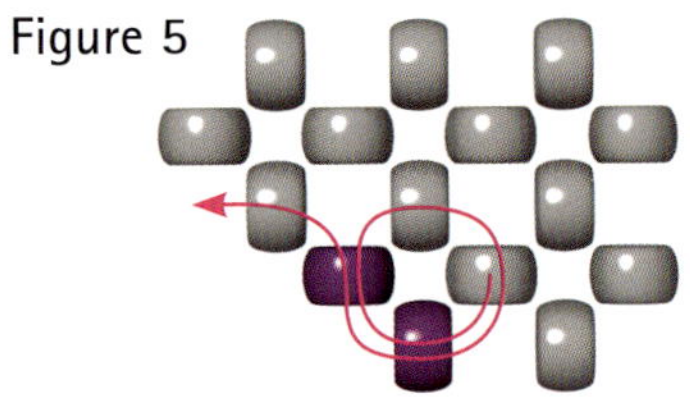

While beading right-angle weave (RAW), the most important thing is to only stitch at right angles. You cannot bead straight ahead.
Four beads are one unit.

Figure 1: Pick up 4 beads and stitch through them to make a circle. This is the first unit.

Figure 2: Pick up 3 beads and stitch through the bead the thread is coming out of and the next two beads. This is the second unit.

Figure 3: Pick up 3 beads and stitch through the bead the thread is coming out of and the next two beads. This is the third unit.

Work in this manner until you reach the desired length. Only the beading direction changes.

Figure 4: To add a second row to the first one, you have to stitch forward to the bead marked green. Pick up 3 beads and stitch through the marked bead and the first added bead.

Figure 5: Pick up 2 beads and stitch through the bead of the previous row, the bead the thread is coming out of and the two beads just added.

Counting units

Four beads are always one unit. But most of them are not only part of one unit, they are part of two units.
The units 1 to 5 are row 1 and units 6 to 10 are row 2.
You can count the units at the upper edge.

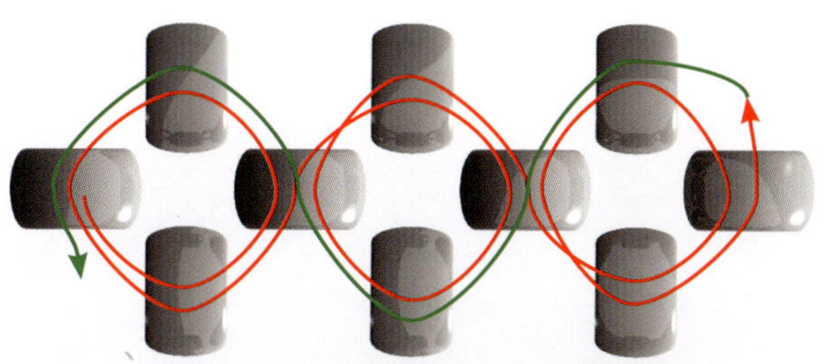

Stitching back

Because of the way you stitch RAW, it always looks a bit messy.
To come to the right position for the next bead, you stitch through half of the beads two times. As you can see in the red thread path, some beads have only one thread and others have two.
When you stitch back along the green thread path, all the beads now have two threads.

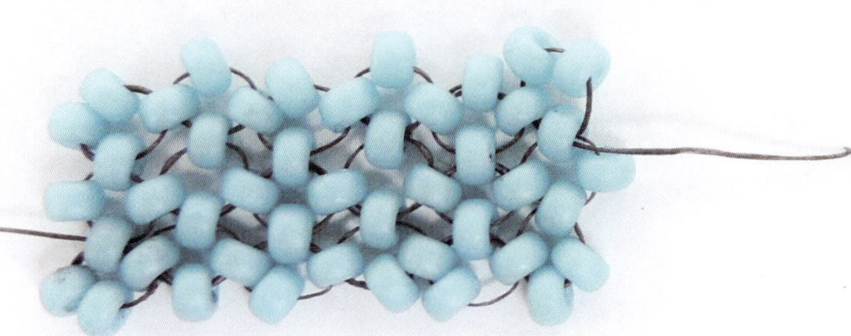

Before stitching back

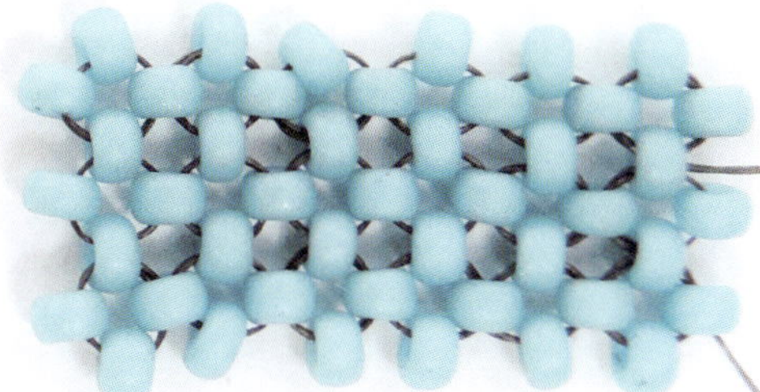

After stitching back

Cubic RAW

Pick up 4 beads and join them to make a circle.

Pick up 3 beads and stitch through the bead the thread is coming out of and the next bead of the basic circle.

Pick up 2 beads and stitch through the first added bead of the last step and the next two beads of the base circle.

Pick up 2 beads and stitch through the first added bead of the last step, the next two beads of the base circle and upward through the last bead added in step 2.

Pick up 1 bead and stitch through the first bead added in the last step, the next bead in the base circle and the two last added beads in step 2.

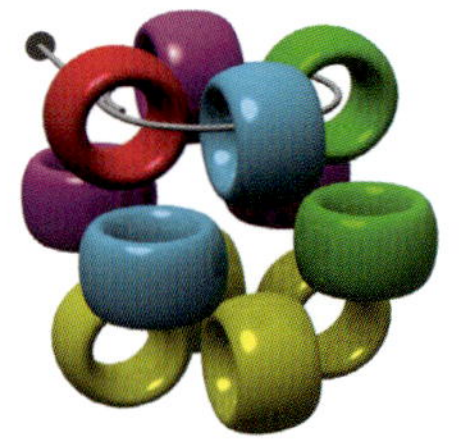

Now stitch through all four top beads, so that they are connected.
This is your first cubic RAW unit - you can bead on in every direction.

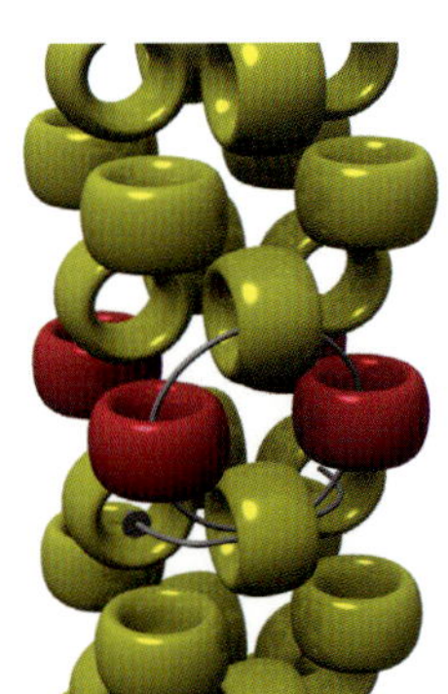

Attaching Cubic RAW

If you want to attach two strands, just add the red beads.

Jump Rings & Eyes

Right

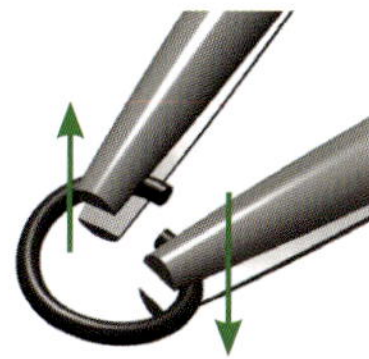

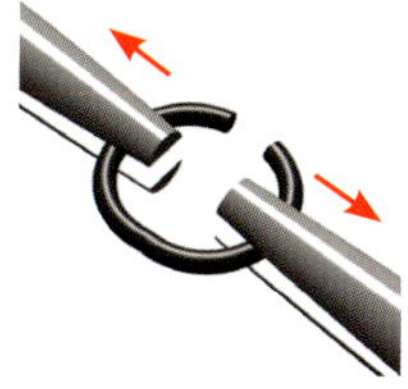

Opening and closing jump rings

Always open a jump ring as the drawing on the far left shows, twisting one side up and one side down.
Never pull a jump ring open left and right.

Figure 1

Figure 2

Making loops

First cut off the excess wire, about 1 cm past the bead. Make sure to cut the wire with the flat side of your wire cutter, so you get a flat end.
Bend the wire a bit beyond 90° (figure 1).
Grasp the end of the wire with your round-nose pliers and bend the eye (figure 2).
If you wish to make a number of loops of identical size, make a little mark on the tip of your pliers with a waterproof marker and line up your wire on that mark each time.

Sprocket from
Beads go Punk!